William Thomson

Memoirs of the Late War in Asia

With a Narrative of the Imprisonment and Sufferings of our Officers...

William Thomson

Memoirs of the Late War in Asia
With a Narrative of the Imprisonment and Sufferings of our Officers...

ISBN/EAN: 9783744750301

Printed in Europe, USA, Canada, Australia, Japan

Cover: Foto ©ninafisch / pixelio.de

More available books at **www.hansebooks.com**

MEMOIRS

OF THE

LATE WAR IN ASIA.

WITH A

NARRATIVE

OF THE

IMPRISONMENT AND SUFFERINGS

OF OUR

OFFICERS AND SOLDIERS:

BY

AN OFFICER of COLONEL BAILLIE's DETACHMENT.

VOL. II.

LONDON:

PRINTED FOR THE AUTHOR;

AND SOLD BY J. MURRAY, FLEET-STREET.

M.DCC.LXXXVIII.

MEMOIRS

OF THE

LATE WAR IN ASIA.

A Narrative of the Captivity and Sufferings of the Officers, Soldiers, and Sepoys, who fell into the Hands of Hyder-Ally, after the Battle of Conjeveram, September 10, 1780.

WHILE the enemy's horse and elephants marched again and again in barbarian triumph over the field of battle, the wounded and bleeding English, who were not instantly trodden to death by the feet of those animals, lingered out a miserable existence, exposed in the day to the burning rays of a vertical sun, and in the night to the ravages of foxes, jackalls, and tygers, allured to that horrid scene by the scent of human

1780.

1780. human blood. Many officers, as well as privates, stripped of all that they had, after protracting hour after hour, and day after day, in pain, miserably perished; others rising, as it were, from the dead, after an incredible loss of blood, which induced for a time the most perfect insensibility and stupefaction, found means to rejoin their friends in chains, with whom they were destined to share, for years, the horrors of the gloomy jail, rendered still more dreadful by frequent apprehensions of that assassination which, they had the most undoubted proofs, had been practised on numbers of their fellow-prisoners, dispersed in different places of confinement, throughout the dominions of a barbarous enemy.

In Europe, the horrors of war are mitigated by the mildness of the climate, and the humanity of the conqueror. In Asia, an inveterate antipathy against Europeans conspires with a dry and parched land, where it is not an easy matter for the sick and wounded to obtain even the comfort of water, and, with the rigours of fervid heat,

to

to prefs down the load of suffering on the defencelefs head of him who has none to help him.

Hyder-Ally, feated in a chair in his tent, enjoyed at Damul, fix miles from the fcene of action, the fight of his prifoners, and the heads of the flain. Colonel Baillie, with feveral other officers, who, like himfelf, were inhumanly wounded, were carried to his camp. The vehicle on which the Colonel was borne was a cannon. While thefe unfortunate gentlemen lay on the ground, in the open air, at Hyder-Ally's feet, heads of their unfortunate friends were, from time to time, prefented to the conqueror; fome of them even by Englifh officers, who were forced to perform that inhuman fervice. One Englifh gentleman, in particular, was forced to carry two heads of his countrymen, which proved to be Captain Phillips and Doctor Wilfon. But, foon after the arrival of the Englifh officers, Hyder, touched with a latent fpark of humanity, ordered the practice of bringing heads before him, while the Englifh gentlemen were

1780. were present, to be discontinued; and the heads of Captain Phillips and Doctor Wilson he ordered to be removed. A dooley was sent to the field of battle in search of Colonel Fletcher; but he could not find him. The Colonel's head was afterwards carried to the barbarian's camp. As some of our officers were obliged to carry the heads of their countrymen to Hyder's camp, so others were obliged to carry heavy loads of firelocks. For every European head that was brought to the barbarian by any of his own people, who were volunteers in that service, a premium was given of five rupees; for every European brought alive ten rupees. The conqueror, enjoying a barbarous triumph over our captive countrymen, suffered them to remain in his presence till sun-set, without ordering them the smallest assistance in their distress. The shell of a tent was then fixed for Colonel Baillie and his officers, but without a bit of straw, or any thing on which they might lie, although repeated application was made for this accommodation, and many of these gentlemen were in danger from their wounds. This tent,

it

it muſt be obſerved at the ſame time, contained only ten perſons; the reſt of the priſoners were obliged to remain in the open air. About ſeven o'clock towards the evening, Colonel Baillie was viſited by Monſieur Goddard, a French officer, who, although in poor circumſtances himſelf, aſſiſted our countrymen to the utmoſt extent of his power. At ten, ſome pilaw was ſent to the priſoners from the Circar.

1780.

Several officers were alſo carried to Tippoo Saib, who treated them with great humanity. He invited them into his tent, gave them biſcuit, and to each five pagodas. One of the gentlemen, Captain Monteith, who was a married man, expreſſed an earneſt deſire of ſending a letter to his wife at Madras; with which Tippoo readily complied. Nothing could be more ſtriking, on this ſad occaſion, than the contraſt between the conduct of the father and that of the ſon.

Hyder-Ally, on the day after the engagement, moved his army from Damul to Muſſalawaulk, where he had left his baggage,

Sept. 11.

1780. gage, with his tents standing, when he marched to attack Colonel Baillie. Some of our wounded officers were carried in palanquins without any covering, exposed to a sultry sun, and many of them were obliged to walk, subjected to the gross abuse, and even to the blows of their several guards. The moment they arrived at the limits of Hyder's camp, they had a pleasing instance of the superior humanity and courtesy of European officers contrasted with the inhumanity of Hyder's people. Fifteen French officers saluted them with the compliment of the hat, and they found the fly of a marqui with a small tent pitched for their reception. Soon after this Captain Pimoran, a French officer, who before the siege of Mahi had been sent from Pondicherry with one hundred and eighty Europeans belonging to the regiment of Lorrain, visited Colonel Baillie, expressed his sorrow at seeing him reduced to his present unhappy situation, and presenting Mr. Lally's best respects, assured him that this commander had applied to Hyder-Ally for leave to visit him, but had been refused. Mahomed-Ally,

one

one of Hyder's principal Generals, was introduced to Colonel Baillie by Dr. Lloyd, who had formerly refided at Madras. Captain Pimoran brought along with him fome clothes, bread, wine, and two French furgeons to drefs the wounded. Several other French officers, too, were very active in adminiftering to the Englifh prifoners the utmoft aid and confolation it was in their power to afford. No pen can do juftice to the humanity of thofe gentlemen, without whofe affiftance many of our officers muft have perifhed: but their merit will for ever be embalmed in the hearts and minds of all who felt or who witneffed their beneficence.

1780.

From Captain Pimoran Colonel Baillie received three hundred pagodas for a bill on Madras, which he diftributed among the officers. Hyder fent five hundred rupees, which the Colonel declined to accept, as being too fmall a fum for diftribution among his officers and foldiers.

On the 12th of September, at twelve o'clock in the afternoon, arrived in Hyder-Ally's camp, at Muffalawaulk, Lieutenant Bowfer

1780. Bowfer and Enfign Dick, with some privates. They were carried to the head Paymafter's, or Buckfhee's tent, close to that of Hyder, where they remained for several hours, stripped of all their clothes, obliged to lie down on a bed of sand, their wounds exposed to a severe sun, and their burning thirst unquenched by a drop of water. On the same day arrived Lieutenant Cox and the Enfigns Maconichy and Wemyfs. These gentlemen had reached Conjeveram, imagining that place to be still in our poffeffion, and thus fell into the hands of the enemy. Lieutenant Bowfer, under the same miftaken notion, was making for the same place, when he was taken by a party of the enemy's horfe.

During the time that this party remained near the Buckfhee's tent, the heads of upwards of ten Europeans were brought by different people, in order to receive the promifed reward. The barbarians were so unfeeling, that many of the heads were thrown on the ground, close to the Englifh officers. At the fame time that many individuals of the loweft caftes, took frequent opportunities

ties of doing and saying every thing that 1780. they conceived to be calculated for the purpose of making impreffions of horror and of fear: if by chance any head-man, or perfons of note happened to come near us, or to have any bufinefs with us, it was, in general, their manner to treat us, not indeed with expreffions of hoftile refentment or execration, but with every mark of difguft and contempt. They would, at the very time they were fpeaking, turn away their heads, and, on fome occafions, communicate their fentiments, and learn ours, by means of a third perfon.

If the horrid fcene, traverfed in this part of our narrative, fhall not offend, but rather intereft the reader, it may be proper to bring it ftill clofer to view, by a particular defcription of the fituation of one or two gentlemen, whofe cafes, chofen as the firft that occurred, bear but too near a refemblance to thofe of their unfortunate fellow-fufferers. Lieutenant Thomas Bowfer, who, before Colonel Baillie difplayed a flag of truce, had received a mufket ball in his leg, after our little army furrendered, which

it

1782. it did about eleven o'clock, received eight desperate wounds with a scymitar. These, as might be expected, brought him to the ground, where he lay deprived of all sensation for seven hours. Towards the evening he awakened from his trance, stripped of all his clothes, except a pair of under drawers, and part of his shirt, with an intense thirst, calling out, and imploring from the enemy a little water. Some, moved by compassion, and yielding to the natural impulse of humanity, forgot their antipathies, and in this extremity of distress, lent their assistance, while others answered his importunate supplications only with reviling language, and threats to put him instantly to death; which he entreated them to do, as there was nothing in reality which he so earnestly wished for. The water which was administered to him by some friendly hand, was deeply tinged with blood. It was brought from a small pool in the field of battle, about fifty or sixty yards from the spot where he lay. In this pool many of our men had been cut down, and others, bleeding and dying, had crawled to it under the impulse of burning thirst. One of Hyder's soldiers was so humane as

to

to furnish Mr. Bowser with an earthen pot, or chatty, holding about a pint, full of the tinged water already described, and, at the same time to inform him where he would find the pool from whence it was taken, advising him to make for it as well as he could. Thither accordingly he crawled; and when he arrived, was struck with horror at the sight of the dead and wounded, with which it was surrounded and filled. He filled his chatty, and endeavoured to proceed towards Conjeveram: but he had not advanced above three or four hundred yards, when he was quite overcome, and obliged to lie all night in the open air, during which there fell two heavy showers of rain.

In the morning of the 11th, he made a second effort to proceed towards Conjeveram; but, after walking about a mile, he was met by some of the enemy's horsemen, who asked him who he was? In the hope that they would think him below their notice, he answered that he was a poor soldier, and that he was going to seek for some relief under his distresses at Conjeveram. They informed

1780. informed him that that place was in the possession of Hyder, and that he must proceed as a prisoner to his camp, taking charge of him at the same time, and obliging him to walk without any assistance. At eight o'clock, the horsemen delivered him up to two of the enemy's sepoys, who behaved to him with rather more humanity and kindness. They gave him water out of the palms of their hands, placed properly together for that purpose; for by this time he had become so stiff with his wounds, that he could not of himself bend or stoop, even in the smallest degree. Whenever he wanted to reach to any thing, the guard, taking hold of his arm, let him gently down and pulled him up. About twelve o'clock, he was equally surprized and overjoyed to come up with a brother officer, Ensign Dick, a quarter-master serjeant of artillery, and two privates. He was now joined to this party, who were nearly in the same situation with himself. The quarter-master serjeant had received so deep a cut across the back part of his neck, that he was obliged to hold his head in his hands, in order to keep it from falling

falling to a side, all the journey. The least 1780. shake or unevenness of the ground made him cry out with pain. He once and again ceased from all attempts to proceed, abandoning himself to the despair of ever being able to accomplish his painful journey, or to prolong his miserable life; but being encouraged, called on, and conjured by his companions to renew his efforts, he did so, and they were succefsful. He recovered of his wound, and is now alive; the most striking proof, perhaps, that is to be found, of that power or principle of recovery and self-preservation which beneficent Providence has implanted in the constitution of our nature. As they moved slowly on, they perceived several Europeans lying dead on the road, and naked; others dying, and many calling out in vain for water. To their prisoners, however, who were able to walk, however slowly, the guards administered a little dry rice soaked in water. They were not indulged with water, as they could not stoop to affist themselves, so often as they wished for it. It was often refused to their most earnest entreaties. Nor were

were they allowed to rest oftener than at the spaces of two or three hundred yards, which appeared to them tedious and painful journies; and permission to rest a little, even after these, was accounted a great favour.

Between eleven and twelve o'clock at night, this little party arrived in Hyder's camp, where they were obliged, as has been observed, to lie on the bare ground, exposed to the winds and rain all night, although there were empty tents at no greater distance than ten yards. They now met with some assistance from certain sepoys, who had formerly been in our service.

On the 12th, as soon as it was day-light, this little party anxiously requested to be sent to Colonel Baillie, and the other officers, but were told that they must be carried before Hyder. An order for this purpose arrived about ten o'clock; and on their way to his tent, they were accosted by several Europeans, who had formerly been in our service, but had deserted. These men sympa-

sympathized with our situation, and insisted 1780. on our drinking a little arrack with them, which we did, in the midst of multitudes who crowded around us. They took their leave of their kind entertainers, whom, in the midst of their own distresses, they could not help considering as unfortunate; but they had not proceeded above an hundred yards before they were ordered to stop. They were at this time so overcome by fatigue, that they laid themselves down on a bed of sand, almost devoured with flies, and a spectacle to thousands of spectators. At this time Captain Pimoran came up to them, took down their names, expressed the greatest sorrow at their distressful situation, and gave to each of them one shirt, one pair of long drawers, one pocket handkerchief, and to each also a pagoda. He farther gave orders that some victuals should be dressed for them. About twelve o'clock another order arrived for them to proceed to Hyder immediately; but on their arrival at the Paymaster's tent, which was close to Hyder's, as already mentioned, they were again ordered to stop, and proceed no farther.

1780. ther. They were now so exceedingly reduced by their accumulated distresses, that there was not one of them who thought it possible they should live much longer, and who was not convinced that he should very soon die. At this time Lieutenant Bowser saw Dr. Lloyd, whom he had formerly known at Madras, coming out of Hyder's tent. He instantly requested one of the guards to call the Doctor, and, after making himself known to him, begged that he would obtain an order that his small party might be sent to Colonel Baillie and the other officers. With this request the Doctor complied, without the smallest delay. There were some of them so exhausted with want, pain, and fatigue, added to previous loss of blood, that it was found necessary that they should be carried on the backs of French soldiers.

On the 13th, Kistna-row, Hyder-Ally's Dewan, or Treasurer, brought a thousand rupees, which Colonel Baillie divided in the following manner :—To each Captain thirteen rupees; to the Lieutenants nine; to the Ensigns seven; and to the non-commissioned officers

officers and privates, one rupee each. This 1780. officer of Hyder's took a lift of our names, and delivered to Colonel Baillie a quantity of filk cloth, palampore, and fome pieces of coarfe cloth. The Colonel gave to the Captains, Surgeons, and Lieutenants of his Majefty's 73d regiment, each a filk cloth; to the fubalterns one piece of coarfe cloth, with one fmall palampore; and to each private one piece of cloth. This day Enfign Wemyfs died. On this day, alfo, a foldier brought the names of Captain Ferrier, Lieutenant Wade, and Enfign Moncrieff, written on a piece of an earthen pot or chatty. Thefe poor gentlemen had taken this method of fignifying that they were ftill alive, and of requefting fome affiftance. Serjeant Macormick, on the day after the engagement, found Lieutenant Wade and Enfign Moncrieff thrown into a bufh full of thorns, and fo defperately wounded, that they were incapable of adminiftering to themfelves, or to one another, the fmalleft relief or affiftance. The ferjeant, not without difficulty, removed thefe unfortunate gentlemen to the fhade of a tree, and having fupplied

1780. supplied them with a little water, left them to the care of Providence. It was not in his power, nor, alas! in ours, to afford to our friends the smallest aid, or to console them under their sufferings, by any token of our sympathetic sorrow at their extreme distress.

Sept. 14.
Some trunks of cloth were sent, by orders from Hyder, for the use of the whole of his prisoners. Colonel Baillie presented the commandant of our guard with an hundred rupees. About eleven in the forenoon Kistna-row, Hyder's treasurer, came and ordered such of us as were capable of walking to stand up. This order was instantly obeyed; and a separation took place. Colonel Baillie, the Captains Baird, Rumley, Lucas, Menteith, and Wragg, with the Lieutenants Lindsey and Frazer, were ordered to remain in the enemy's camp. The officers not wounded, who amounted to the number of twenty-three, were sent to Bangalore; and those who were wounded, of whom there were twenty-seven, to Arneé. The wounded privates were in like manner sent to Arneé,

neé, and thofe not wounded to Bangalore. 1780 All this was done fo fuddenly on the part of Hyder, that we had not fo much as an opportunity of fpeaking to each other, and if any one had dared to folicit this privilege, he would undoubtedly have been treated by the guards, who were under the neceffity of carrying their mafter's orders into prompt execution, with great abufe. However, as they could not prevent us from feeing, we beheld our brother fufferers mounted on fmall horfes called tattoos: and foon after this, fome doolies were brought for the party deftined for Arneé, who were hurried into them with every mark of contempt. Thefe doolies are the moft inhuman vehicles in which Europeans were ever placed. The common fort of them are from three feet and an half to four feet long, and about two feet and an half broad. They are compofed of a frame made of bamboo or common wood, with four pofts at the corners, to which the fides and ends are faftened, at the diftance of eight inches from the ground. To each of thefe pofts is fixed a ftraight bamboo,

1780. bamboo, or large pole, by means of which the machine is carried by four coolies or bearers. The frame is lashed together by ropes made of the fibres of the cocoa nut, and sometimes by small rattan canes, which, at the same time that they serve to fasten the machine, supply the place of a seat. The doolies are usually covered over with coarse cotton cloth; but as ours had no coverings of any kind, many of our gentlemen suffered very severely.

The poor soldiers, who laboured under every misery, were some of them put into these doolies, and above fifty of them placed on arrack bandiers or carts. It is impossible to describe the inexpressible sufferings of those unfortunate men, desperately wounded, their bodies exposed to a severe sun, placed six or eight of them together on these arrack bandiers, knocking against each other from the jolting of the machine, and refused even a drop of water. When we had advanced, in this painful manner, about four miles from Hyder's camp, we made an halt.

halt. A fly of a *marqui* was now pitched, 1780. to fhelter us from the weather. About eight in the evening there fell an heavy fhower of rain, which proved fo deftructive to fome of the foldiers that they died raving mad: for thefe poor men having neither tent nor covering of any kind, the water penetrated even to the cerebellum, through the fractures of the fkull. About twelve o'clock at night a fheep was brought, with fome rice, and dreffed by our fervants.

Doctor Campbell, one of our furgeons, being at the point of death, requefted leave to bid his laft farewel to his brother, who was with the Bangalore party, encamped at the diftance from us of about an hundred yards. His requeft, after a good deal of hefitation, was granted.

At fun-rife we were ordered to eat fome cold rice, and about eight o'clock we moved onward to Scolore; at which place we arrived about five in the afternoon. Captain Ferrier, and feveral privates, died here, and Sept. 15.

were

1780. were thrown carelessly into an hole close by us. The dooley boys, of the hill or cannery cast, during the course of our journey thither, behaved to us in a most barbarous manner, often beating us with sticks, refusing to give us water, and wantonly and cruelly exposing us to the sun. At any time when we were permitted to halt for a little rest and refreshment, if they had an opportunity of setting us down under the shade of a grove or tree, they would give themselves trouble to expose us to suffering, by carrying us about to that side of the grove or tree where we should not enjoy the cooling shade of their leafy branches, but suffer the rage of the noon-day sun, in its utmost rigor.—The men who carried these doolies, as well as some others of the lower casts of people in Hyder's dominions, would frequently revile us in terms not to be repeated. They would tell us, that we should be forced to eat our own dung*, and express

---

* It would appear, from the sacred writings of the Old Testament, that this expression of hatred and aversion was, in antient times, common in other parts of the East.

their

their hopes and confidence, that when we 1780.
fhould arrive at the place of our deftination,
Hyder would not fail to put us to death.

We moved off this day at the fame time Sept.
as yefterday, and reached Arneé (which, 16.
with the adjacent country, had taken choul,
or come under the protection of Hyder)
at three in the afternoon. Here we were
crammed together into a filthy dungeon,
barely fufficient to receive us. Lieutenant
Cotton, juft as he entered within the prifon
dropped down dead. It is probable, that
had we not halted at Arneé, the whole of us
would have perifhed. In the evening fome
rice was fent to us, with a little maffal,
which is a fpecies of fpice, or pepper.

Our daily allowance at Arneé was to each Sept.
of us one fear of rice, and fometimes a little 17.
lean mutton, one fpoonful of ghee, a fmall
quantity of curry ftuff, half a fpoonful of
falt, and two or three fticks of firewood.—
Our fervants were allowed each three cafh
per day, and one fear of rice with a little
B 4 falt,

1780. salt. Application was made for a little straw to sleep on, but without success. We were forced to rest on the bare ground, without wine, tea, sugar, or any other comfort or refreshment than has been already specified.

At the time of our leaving Hyder's camp, Monsieur Castro, a surgeon, came with two or three rusty instruments, and attended us, during our stay at Arneé. Monsieur Castro, it is justice to say, shewed us great humanity and attention. Our only medicine was a composition of wax and oil, which was purchased in Hyder's camp.

Sept. 18. In the evening died Doctor Campbell. The death of this gentleman was an object of sincere regret to all the prisoners. Application was made to the Keeladar for some cloth for bandages. This necessary article being refused, we were obliged to tear up the piece of coarse cloth we had received as a present from Hyder. Many of us were under the necessity of going, for several days, naked,

naked, being in poffeffion of only one fhirt 1780. and troufers, which, having already worn them fix days, we were obliged to get wafhed. Shoes we had none. We had nothing of any kind to fupply the place of either bedding or bed-cloaths; and the rain, falling on us through the crazy roof of our prifon, difturbed and annoyed us by night and by day. We were this day vifited by an Hungarian ferjeant in the fervice of Hyder. This man, although he was as great a rogue as could be imagined, proved afterwards of very great fervice to us. After repeated applications to the Keeladar we at laft received, on this day, five old mats, and made a divifion of them by cutting them in pieces: but they were fo bad that we could fcarcely ufe them.

We applied to the Keeladar, chiefly on Sept. account of the wounds that many of us had 19. received in our heads, for a barber. He returned for anfwer, that if we troubled him any more, he would fend us irons.

This

1780. Sept. 20.   This day was marked by the death of Mr. John Baillie a cadet:

22.   As this was by that of Enfign Dick:

29.   And this by that of Lieutenant Cox.

Mr. Baillie, during the courfe of the preceding night, had fallen into a delirium; and as we were not allowed any light in our prifon, he walked over feveral of the wounded officers, who, in the greateft anguifh, cried out in vain for affiftance. We had thefe gentlemen as decently carried out as our fituation would allow. However, we learned afterwards, that they were ftripped of the piece of cloth which covered them, and thrown into the bed of a river, expofed to jackalls and tygers and other ravenous animals.

Oct. 4.   Enfign Gordon, who had now recovered from his wounds, was taken out of prifon and fent to Scringapatam. Lieutenant Mackay received fifty pagodas fent by our refident resident at Pondichery, Mr. Skardon, and conveyed to us by means of our good friend the French doctor. This gentleman, touched with our miserable situation, carried a letter to the humane, to the godlike Captain Pimoran, whose name it is impossible to mention without the liveliest emotions of gratitude, admiration, and love, attending his duty in Hyder's army, employed at that time in the siege of Arcott, which is distant from Arneé about eighteen English miles. The goodness of the doctor was the greater that he undertook and performed this friendly journey, notwithstanding the mean insinuations of the Hungarian serjeant abovementioned, who assured him that he would undoubtedly be detected, and dragged to death at an elephant's foot. Captain Pimoran presented his sincere respects, and begged leave to assure us, that he had sent all the ready money in his possession by Monsieur Castro, but that he would on every occasion assist us to the the utmost of his power. If we had not been favoured with these supplies from this generous Frenchman, a private friend though a public foe, the greater part

1780. Oct. 27.

1780. part of us must have perished through want.

Soon after this we received the melancholy tidings that Captain Pimoran had fallen before Arcott. An honourable death secured to this generous spirit the glory of a life that was an honour to human nature. But we felt inexpressible regret, that we could no longer indulge the hope of testifying, by some visible token, that inward gratitude and esteem which had been awakened in each of our breasts, by his generous goodness.

About this time, the Doctor, having represented to us the miserable situation of our unfortunate soldiers, we purchased for their relief twenty-seven pieces of cloth: but on applying to the Keeladar for permission to send them, we received no answer to our request. So that the sufferings of the poor soldiers remained unassuaged by the comforts which their friends had provided. Nor was this the only, or the most pressing request that we were under the necessity of making

making to our enemies. Our place of retirement, which was fituated within the walls of our difmal dungeon, became fo offenfive, that we made the moft importunate applications to have it cleared. But no orders were iffued for this neceffary fervice by the Keeladar, and none were to be found who would do it voluntarily. The fufferings that arofe from this putrid fource, in a fultry climate, to men afflicted and worn down with fluxes; the fwarms of odious vermin that affailed our naked and fore bodies, and that, penetrating and neftling in the wounded ear of a certain officer, turned the auricular nerve into an inftrument of the moft exquifite pain for feveral nights and days: thefe cannot be recollected without horrour, nor related without difguft. Nor is it worth while, after hinting at fuch diftreffes as thefe, to relate that in the prifon of Arneé many of the Englifh officers, on account of the want of fervants, were obliged to wafh their own pots, to kindle their own fires, and drefs their own victuals.

1780.

At

1780. At this period of our Narrative, it may be proper to give the following statement of the different fates that awaited the gentlemen of Colonel Baillie's detachment, in the late unfortunate action near Tacoallum.

Names of Corps.	Killed	Wounded.	Died of Wounds.
Lieut. Col. Baillie		1	
Lieut. Col. Fletcher	1		
Lieut. Frazer, Brigadier Major			
Lieut. Read, Aid de Camp			
Lieut. Chace, Brigadier Major		1	
Ensign Burgier, Commissary	1		
SURGEONS.			
Mr. Wilson	1		
Raine		1	
Campbell			1
Ogilvie			
Grenadier Company, 73d Regiment.			
Lieut. John Lindsey		1	
Lieut. Gusin	1		
Mr. Forbes, Volunteer	1		
Light Infantry, 73d.			
Capt. David Baird		1	
Lieut. Mackenzie	1		
Lieut. Melville		1	
Mr. Hodges, Volunteer			
Mr. Cuthbert, Ditto		1	
Carry over	6	7	1

Names of Corps.	Killed	Wounded	Died of Wounds	1780.
Brought over	6	7	1	
Company's Artillery.				
Capt. Jones				
Lieut. Smith		1		
Lieut. Cox			1	
Lieut. Mirton	1			
Mr. Monie, Conductor	1			
Capt. Phillips's European Grenadiers.				
Capt. Phillips	1			
Lieut. Knox			1	
Lieut. Maffey		1		
Enfign Clarke	1			
Capt. Ferrier's European Grenadiers.				
Capt. Ferrier			1	
Lieut. Wade	1			
Lieut. M'Neale				
Lieut. Bowfer		1		
Lieut. Halliburton		1		
John Goree, Volunteer				
John Hope, ditto		1		
—— Latham, ditto				
Sepoy Markfmen.				
Lieut. Muat.				
Two Companies of European Infantry.				
Capt. Menteith		1		
Capt. Wragg				
Carry over	11	13	4	

1780.

Names of Corps.	Killed	Wounded.	Died of Wounds
Brought over	11	13	4
Enfign Galway	1		
Lieut. Nafh		1	
Lieut. Dring			
Mr. Baillie, Volunteer		1	
Lieut. Baillie, Volunteer			
Five Companies Sepoy Grenadiers.			
Capt. Rumley		1	
Enfign Moore		1	
Enfign Maconichy		1	
Enfign Stringer		1	
Enfign Wood	1		
Enfign Clarke	1		
Five Companies Sepoy Grenadiers.			
Capt. Gowdie		1	
Lieut. Mackay		1	
Enfign Picklaw		1	
Enfign Wilfon		1	
Enfign Gordon		1	
Enfign Sheddon	1		
Firft Carnatic Battalion.			
Capt. Lucas		1	
Lieut. Campbell			
Enfign Innis		1	
Enfign Macalifter		1	
Enfign MacLane	1		
Enfign Lombard	1		
Enfign Corner			
Enfign Lang			
Carry over	17	27	4

Names of Corps.	Killed.	Wounded.	Died of Wounds.	1780.
Brought over	17	27	4	
Second Circar Battalion.				
Capt. Powell	1			
Lieut. Cotton		1		
Lieut. Forbes				
Lieut. Jurin		1		
Enfign Curtis	1			
Enfign Hemming	1			
Enfign Dawes	1			
EnfignWynn	1			
Enfign Dick			1	
Enfign Forbes		1		
Second Carnatic Battalion.				
Capt. Geo. Nixon	1			
Lieut. Butler				
Lieut. Dalrymple		1		
Enfign Mackay		1		
Enfign Bofwell	1			
Enfign Rogers	1			
Enfign Tomlinfon	1			
Enfign Frank				
Six Companies of the 7th Carnatic Battalions				
Capt. Grant		1		
Enfign White				
Enfign Mahagan	1			
Enfign Marfhall	1			
Enfign Macleod	1			
Total	29	32	6	

Vol. II.   C   The

1780. The officers, including volunteers, were in whole eighty-six. Of these seventy were killed or wounded, and only sixteen escaped unhurt.

Nov. 1. The following gentlemen being recovered of their wounds were sent off to Seringapatam: Lieutenants Massey, Turin, Chace; Ensigns Wilson and Stringer. This day we received accounts of the Pittah of Arcott having surrendered.

Dec. 8. The following gentlemen being recovered of their wounds, were ordered for Seringapatam, and previously to their departure made up a sum of one hundred and fifty pagodas, in bills on Madras, for the French Doctor, their worthy and good friend, who shed tears on their departure:—Captain Grant; the Lieutenants Bowser, Butler, Mackay; Ensigns, Picklaw, Moore, Maconichy, Macalister; Volunteers Baillie and Hope. Lieutenants Melvill, Dalrymple, and Knox, were left at Arneé. Mr. Knox laboured under a dropsy, nor had the Doctor any instruments to give him relief.

lief. Lieutenant Melvill had received a shot in his left arm, which broke and shattered the bone; and, a few inftants after, as he was in the act of turning round to fpeak to fome of the foldiers, a ball paffed through the fame arm, and part of his left breaft. Had it not been for the accident of turning round, this ball muft inevitably have put an end to his exiftence. The enemy's cavalry having broke into our ranks, in the confufion and carnage which enfued, the bone of his right arm was cut in two by a fabre, and he was dafhed unmercifully on the ground. He was, after this, ftripped of all his clothes, even of his fhirt, and while he was dragged to a convenient fpot for this purpofe, his head ftriking againft every ftone, and his disjointed arms trailing over the enfanguined foil, he fuffered the extremity of pain. As he lay naked, bleeding and helplefs on this fpot, an horfeman, with wanton cruelty, wounded him in the back with his fpear. In this miferable fituation he lay for two days and two nights, expofed to the tortures of a burning fun, to the danger of being torn to pieces by beafts of prey,

1780.

1780. prey, and, what every soldier whose fate it has been to lie wounded on a field of battle knows to be more dreadful than any or all other circumstances of suffering united; to the want of water. Lieutenant Melvill having made repeated efforts to assuage, in some degree, his burning thirst, by means of whatever grass or herbs was within the narrow circumference of his reach, in vain, was reduced, like other men in similar situations of extreme distress, to the necessity of seeking for relief from the moisture of his own body. Had it not been for the humane and most generous attentions of Lieutenant Forbes, who lay by him part of the first night and assisted him, he must in all human probability have perished. He was, at last, on the morning of the third day, picked off the field by some of the enemy, who, without any circumstance of fellow-feeling or humanity, carried him in a rude and cruel manner to their camp. The recovery of Mr. Melvill may be ranked among the most striking proofs of the provision that is made for the preservation of the human frame.

We

We left Arneé about nine in the morning, penetrated with forrow at parting from our friends and fellow-fufferers. We were under charge of a Bramin, one Commandant of the troops, confifting of a few firelock men, one hundred and fifty colleries, and a few horfemen. Piats, or fmall horfes, were given for our conveyance. A horfe-keeper was allowed to each piat horfe, who had a rope faftened to the head ftall of the bridle, with pofitive orders not to quit his ftation. The whole of us were ordered to move on in a rank entire. We fuffered much from this mode of conveyance, having only a pad in the room of a faddle, and no ftirrups; crowds of people gazing at us, and many behaving in a moft infolent manner. When we arrived on the glacis, we met thirty-two of our unfortunate foldiers hand-cuffed, two and two, barefoot, and almoft naked. Every exertion on our part was made, in order to alleviate their diftrefs.

1780.

We arrived in Poloor about four in the afternoon. Some rice was boiled for us and the foldiers, with a little falt. The rice, after being boiled, was rolled into a ball for the

1780. the soldiers, about the size of a foot-ball, and each person received his ball. The soldiers, at the different halting places, were kept separate from us. As many of these were not recovered from their wounds, they were allowed, after repeated applications, to attend the surgeons of the country; but under particular restrictions not to ask for news. Many of the soldiers suffered much from the want of shoes. These men not being able to walk, bullocks were provided, on which they were forced to ride, still remaining hand-cuffed to their comrades. This piece of cruelty we pointed out both to the Bramin and Commandant; but only received for answer, that they had no orders from the Bahauder to take off their irons. Whenever we approached near a village, tom-toms, a kind of drums, and winding collery horns, advanced in front, that the inhabitants might, by this discordant music, be assembled together to gaze at us, as we passed through. We suffered much, during our march, from the intense heat, as they would not travel in the night, but only in the day time, and that during the hottest part of it. The daily allowance which we received

received was one small sheep, divided between us and the soldiers, in all forty-one persons, one sear of rice each, with a little salt. In the villages through which we passed, some of the people would express sentiments of compassion, and suffer us to drink water, not indeed out of their vessels, which would have been pollution, but out of the palms of their hands; while others would revile us, and pray that we might be put to the sword without mercy. Such is the extreme difference of natural tempers.

1780.

Arrived at Bangalore, and visited by the Keeladar, who made us many flattering promises, but executed none.

Dec. 18.

About five in the evening arrived at Seringapatam, where we were led in triumph to Hyder's Palace, surrounded by crowds of people, till near seven o'clock, during which time our names were taken down in writing by the Keeladar, and then ordered to a small confined prison, where we found Captains Baird, Wragg, Menteith; Lieutenants Lindsey, Massey, Chace, Turin; Ensigns Wilson and Stringer. Our joy on this oc-

23.

casion

1780. cafion was great; we were allowed one gold fanam each per day, and a French furgeon to attend us (Monfieur Fortuno). The guards here confifted of two goloks (civilians who acted as field deputies), two havaldars, twelve Sepoys, one duffadar, and twelve collerees, a lower clafs of foldiers. Our fervants were permitted to attend the Buzar morning and evening, and allowed by the Keeladar to purchafe one bottle and two thirds of pia arrack, (a liquor diftilled from the bark of a tree), weekly, for each gentleman, the amount of which was one fanam and eight dubs. The poor foldiers who accompanied us were fent to a different prifon.

Enfign Gordon, who left Arneé the 4th of October, was amongft the foldiers here, and in irons. Repeated applications were made to the Myar, or Town Major, to remove him to us, in vain: but at laft, on our folemn affurances that he was an officer, his irons were taken off.

The following are the ftages at which we halted, in our journey from Arneé to
Seringa-

Seringapatam, with the intermediate dif- 1-80.
tances:

	Cofs.	Miles.
From Arneé to Poloor *	6	13¼
A deferted villa	6	13½
Changama -	6	13¼
Chingerry Pett	6	13½
Matore -	6	13¼
Covey Patam †	5	11¼
Ria Cotah -	8	20
Taalcondah -	4	10
Uffore ‡ -	4	10
Bangalore § -	10	25
Carry over	61	144

* This is a very pleafant little village. We were lodged in the ruins of an old palace.

† This place is fituated in the midft of a beautiful and highly cultivated valley, and within fight of the Kiftna Gurry hills. We halted here a whole day, in order to have our cloaths wafhed. The Keeladar, who came and fmoaked his hooker with us, converfed familiarly, and expreffed great compaffion for our misfortunes.

‡ A pleafant little town, furrounded by a ftrong ftone wall, with turrets, and fituated in the midft of extenfive paddy fields.

§ This town is five or fix miles in circumference, well watered, interfperfed with pleafant gardens and groves, and environed by fields and pafture lands of great fertility. It is furrounded by a ftrong ftone wall, and contains a pettah enclofed within a mud wall.

Kin-

1780.

	Cofs.	Miles.
Brought over	61	144
Kingerry Catah	6	15
Ramgurry	8	20
Chenapatam *	4	10
Guutall †	7	$17\frac{1}{2}$
Seringapatam	8	20
	94	$226\frac{1}{2}$

Each cofs is $2\frac{1}{4}$ Englifh miles.   Eng. Miles.

Dec. 23. Repeated applications have been made to the Keeladar, for cots to fleep on, but without fuccefs. We are therefore neceffitated to make ufe of ftraw. The Keeladar will

* At this place we were lodged under a gateway, on each fide of which a gallery was conftructed, fupported by two or three pillars. The foldiers were placed in one of thefe galleries, and the officers in another; which afforded a fcene not more fingular than fatisfactory. For here we had an opportunity of converfing with the poor foldiers, as well as with Enfign Gordon, and indulging our curiofity, by putting a thoufand queftions concerning their fate, and that of others. At parting, we had the pleafure of contributing to their relief and comfort, by furnifhing them with a few cloaths and fome tobacco.

† At Guutall we were lodged in a fmall Choultry. Here we were permitted to go on the ramparts, and to furvey the country, which is very rich, highly cultivated, full of cocoa-nut trees, groves, fields abounding with grain, and well built and populous villages.

not

not even allow the door of the prison to be 1780.
kept open during the course of the day, in
order to admit a little air, although we have
often told him of the dangerous confe-
quences to be apprehended from its exclu-
sion, and also informed him that several
gentlemen were very much indisposed. To
all our reprefentations and fupplications we
received for anfwer, that if any of us died,
they would carry us out lashed to a bamboo,
for the prey of the tygers and jackalls.

An head Bramin belonging to the Circar, 1781.
ordered us all to turn out of our births, and, Jan.
after affembling us near his perfon, attempt- 19.
ed to engage us in the fervice of Hyder,
with the flattering promifes of great pay,
horfes, palanquins, women, flaves, &c. On
our refufing to take fervice, he faid, we
were fine men, and that it grieved him to
fee us in that fituation. He affured us, that
when he invited us to take fervice, it was
not underftood that we fhould fight againft
our country; and that we were to do nothing but walk about at our pleafure.

Received

1781.
Jan.
22.

Received the following letter, brought in privately:

To Captain Wragg.

" Dear Friend,

" I shall never forget you at Combi-
" tore. You was my Enſign; you behaved
" yourſelf to the Company honourably. I
" am ſorry to hear of your being priſoner.
" Pray be ſo good as to take in patience for
" twelve years, two men, being priſoners in
" Seringapatam. The two men are Samuel
" Spencer and John Wilton, both London
" born. We were taken at Errod, in
" 1768. I hope your honour will be ſo
" good as to acquaint the Commander of
" Madras about us two captives, if God
" gives liberty for your honours to return
" back.

(Signed)
" SAMUEL SPENCER,
" JOHN WILTON."

Theſe two unfortunate men, as we learned afterwards, are by trade armourers. They have

have each of them five gold fanams a day, 1781. with two drams of arrack: but they have guards over them, and appear quite dejected. They are allowed to drefs in the European ftyle, but are very dirty.

Arrived Captain Menteith's fervant from Arneé, and informed us of the fall of Fort Gingee, and the death of Lieutenant Knox.

Raifed by fubfcription, and fent to Enfign Jan. Gordon, eight and a half pagodas. 29.

Arrived this afternoon, Captain Lucas and Enfign Macauley; the latter taken at Gingee.

Arrived Lieutenant Colonel Baillie, Cap- Mar. tain Rumley, and Lieutenant Frazer: the 8. two firft of thefe gentlemen in irons, as they alfo had been during their journey from Arcott to this place, which is upwards of two hundred and forty Englifh miles; they were lodged in a veranda, an open gallery, oppofite to our prifon, at the diftance of about two hundred yards. Arrived

1781. rived at the same time Mr. Skardon, resident at Pondicherry, Mr. Brunton, late an Ensign in the Company's service, and a Mr. MacNeal, mate of a country ship; the two last sent amongst the soldiers, and Mr. Skardon to our prison, with the daily allowance of six cash, one seer of rice, half a seer of doll, and a little ghee: this allowance was poor indeed, but as we were on every occasion ready with our small pittance to assist our brother sufferers, we made a monthly subscription in order to put him on a level with us.

Mar. 28. Visited by the Keeladar, who behaved to us in a most contemptuous manner, refusing to speak but through an interpeter. He was very particular in examining our irons.

29. Ordered to be mustered three times a day.

May 3. Visited by a black Commandant, who played a game at chess with Captain Lucas: this game was brought from India into Europe.

Several

Several letters taken by the French doctor's servant for our friends in the Carnatic, requesting a supply of money, and to know if there was any prospect of peace.
1781.
May 4.

The whole of us (except Captain Baird of the 73d) put in heavy irons; and the French surgeon ordered not to attend us. Each pair of irons was from eight to nine pound weight. This was the commencement of a deliberate system, as afterwards more fully appeared, for cutting us off!— This a melancholy day.
10.

Arrived Lieutenant Coke, and put in irons. He was taken at Pandanalore, in the Tanjore country.
20.

Lieutenant Turin's irons taken off, on account of a wound in his thigh.
24.

In consequence and in honour of his Majesty's birth-day, we had for dinner fowl, cutlets, and a flower pudding, and
June 4.

drank

drank his health in a chatty of sherbet.

Aug. 6. Arrived prisoners, five Europeans, with a number of Carnatic slave boys and girls torn from our country.

28. We received accounts of the French doctor's servant having returned from the Carnatic: but no letters from our friends.

Sept. 7. Mr. Christie, serjeant of the Bengal detachment, arrived this afternoon. He belonged to Colonel Pearce's detachment, and was taken prisoner near Pulicat the 3d of August. Mr. Christie, when it was discovered that he was not an officer, was on the 9th sent among the soldiers. Favourable accounts received at this time of the spirited exertions of Mr. Hastings diffuse a general joy throughout the prison.

10. Several gentlemens legs are found to be very much swelled on account of the weight of their irons. - Repeated applications to the

the Keeladar to have them taken off, but without succefs. 1781.

A grand Gentoo feaft, at which the King of Myfore was prefent, a lad about twelve years of age. This royal prifoner is allowed to appear in public only at this particular time. We were allowed, as a very particular favour, to indulge our curiofity with a fight of his majefty. Sept. 18.

Vifited by a Commandant, who afked a few trifling queftions. Oct. 4.

The guard very particular in examining our irons at the different mufters.

A Sepoy of our guard informs us, that fixteen foldiers had been taken out of one of the prifons in Seringapatam and circumcifed, and that they intended to remove fome of us for the fame purpofe.

This evening we faw the Europeans at exercife, and dreffed in the Mahomedan fafhion, 28.

1780. shion, corresponding in number with the Sepoy's information.

Our servants, and those who attended the soldiers, met together every day, in order to receive their daily allowance of rice. Hence we had an opportunity of corresponding with our fellow-captives in the different prisons by means of a rice cake, or hopper, and a cherool or sagar, which is some leaves of tobacco rolled up in the form of a tube so as to be smoked without the aid of a pipe or any other instrument. One would ask another if he would eat a bit of hopper. The person who offered this refreshment took care to give that part of the cake which contained the letter.— In like manner one would ask another for a sagar: and the other, understanding the meaning of the request, would give him what he wanted, if any intelligence was to be communicated: if not, he would perhaps say that he had none. In this manner we had an opportunity of interchanging sentiments, of condoling with one another, and of contributing what little was in our power

to

to the relief of those who were in the greatest want or distress. The consolation we felt in this intercourse of sympathetic affection induced us even to encounter the danger of death; for this most assuredly would have been our lot if our correspondence had been discovered.

In one or other of the conveyances just described, received the following letter from Serjeant Hollingsworth.

" This morning I was informed of
" your being desirous to know in what
" manner the sixteen Europeans were sepa-
" rated from us. On the 18th of Septem-
" ber the head Myar with a Bramin came to
" our prison and ordered the serjeant to call
" in the men, which was immediately done
" without any suspicion, and the above
" Myar and Bramin singled out sixteen of
" the youngest, knocked off their irons, and
" marched them to the Keeladar, and then
" asked if they would take service; when
" they all declared they would sooner die
" than be bound to the service of a tyrant.

"At

1780. "At sun-set they were conducted, one by
"one, to a small apartment, where an
"operator attended, with six caffres to hold
"them while they were circumcised.—
"This was affirmed by them to Ensign
"Brunton.

"This morning the Bramin came into
"our prison again for a drum and fife, but
"they being sick he went away without
"them."

Received the following letter, addressed to Captain Lucas and the officers in our prison, from Serjeant Dempster of the Bengal artillery, who voluntarily entered into the service of Hyder, and who had once on a former occasion deserted from Colonel Pearce's detachment:

"Sir,
"Your servants casting an eye to one
"of us sometime ago, gives us reason to
"think that you would be desirous to
"know something of our present unheard-
"of and unfortunate situation: not to be
"paralleled perhaps in the history or an-
"nals

" nals of any nation. On Wedenſday the 1781.
" 19th of September the Bramin and My-
" ar came to our priſon, and after falling in
" the men, he ſelected ſixteen from the reſt,
" ſmiths being prepared to knock off their
" irons, without giving us the ſmalieſt idea
" of what was to enſue, and conducted us
" to the kutcherce, where they informed us
" upon what account we were releaſed,
" and in a very flattering manner requeſted
" of us to take ſervice. All their promiſes
" and tenders were rejected with diſdain.—
" They then changed their accent, and
" threatened us in the ſevereſt manner.—
" We were then conducted to a large ſquare,
" the repoſitory or ſeminary of thoſe Car-
" natic boys that had been brought into
" ſlavery, whom you ſee every night at ex-
" ercife. Upon our arrival there, how
" great was our ſurpriſe to find two Engliſh
" lads amongſt theſe boys, who had been
" circumciſed three months before our ar-
" rival, one of whom is a Mr. Clarke, who
" had been an Enſign in the 2d batallion,
" 2d regiment; the other a private in the
" ſame regiment. They informed us imme-

D 3 " diately

"diately that we should be circumcised.—
"They had scarce finished telling us this,
"when the guard came in, accompanied by a
"barber*. You, sir, who have delicate feel-
"ings, will conceive what our situation was,
"dragged to what every Christian in the
"universe utterly abhors, and surrounded
"by enemies whose very souls are many
"thousand times blacker than their visage.
"After some resistance on the part of every
"one of us, we were obliged at last to sit
"down and be shaved, after which we re-
"mained in the most cruel uncertainty for
"three or four hours, when our ill-favour-
"ed guard brought us a doze of † majum
"each, and obliged us to to take it. It
"wrought differently. Some were insen-
"sible: others were not. A little after sun-
"set, a black surgeon, with thirty or forty
"caffres, seized and held us while the
"operation was performed. We remained
"under cure for a month, upon six cash
"per day, with mutton, rice, &c. The

* The Mahometans are always shaved all over before circumcision.
† A stupifying drug.

"30th

" 30th of October, we were conducted to 1781.
" the kutcheree, and there examined if we
" would take thofe Carnatic flave boys
" and learn them their difcipline, for which
" we fhould receive each of us one gold
" fanam per day, with provifions and cloaths;
" which we hope, in our prefent fituation,
" you will not conftrue into any difaffection
" to our couhtry or officers, it being all
" force and conftraint.

" However, actuated by lively, and at the
" fame time pungent forrow, that you in your
" prefent diftreffed fituation, fhould be a me-
" lancholy witnefs of thofe men, who were
" fo lately under your command, whofe in-
" dulgence and paternal care, particularly on
" the day of action, was fecond to that of none;
" we humbly make bold to affure you, that
" fcarce filial duty can be exceeded on our
" part, every man in the other prifon and
" here, being at any time ready to lay down
" their lives to refcue you from the fmalleft
" harm. Our fondnefs was the reafon of our
" running this hazard in writing, and moft
" heartily and fincerely wifhing to fee you

D 4 " fhortly

1781. "shortly releafed, and in a way of releafing
"us unfortunate victims from the chains of
"this barbarian.
                (Signed)
        " JOHN MAXWELL DEMPSTER.

    " Once an Enfign in his Majefty's 19th
    " regiment of foot, and late a Serjeant
    " in the Bengal artillery." *

Oct. 30. Duncan Macintofh and Donald Stewart, privates, both of the 73d regiment, were forcibly taken out and circumcifed.

This day Captain Wragg received the following letter;

" Sir,
    " AFTER the many repeated favours I
    " have received at your hands, I think it
    " my duty to acquaint you of my prefent.
    " fituation; that I am unfortunately one of
    " the men who was taken out, and under-
    " went the dreadful pain of circumcifion.
                (Signed)
        ." BENTALL WOODLEY."

                                    * Captain

Captain Baird put in irons.

1781.
Nov. 10.

A report prevails that our correspondence with the different prisons is discovered, which gives the greatest alarm. We proceed instantly to destroy or to conceal papers, knives, scissars, razors, &c. This journal, which was written within a very small compass, on a slip of Indian paper, in such an hand as that in which innocent idlers write out the Lord's prayer within the circumference of a halfpenny, was concealed on this, as on other occasions of alarm, which were not unfrequent, in a small hole dug deep in the earthen floor of our prison, carefully filled up and beaten into a perfect equality and resemblance of the contiguous surface.

11.

It is reported that a man was intercepted who had undertaken to carry a letter from us to Colonel Baillie.

12.

Having made repeated application for medicines for the sick, we were informed that

1781. that the strictest orders had been issued, that no medicines should be administered to us by any person, under the pain of the most severe and shocking mutilation. We had not come there to live, we were told; and that nothing could be more acceptable to the Nabob than the news of our death. These melancholy tidings had a visible effect on the minds of the gentlemen who were indisposed. Cut off from all hope of relief, but that alone which might possibly arise from the unassisted efforts of nature, they began to droop and despond exceedingly. We repeated and pressed our solicitations for medicines to no purpose. The sentries to whom we applied, declared, that they would willingly bring in some, if they could do it with safety; but that their orders were express, and that their ears and noses, and right hands, must pay the forfeiture of disobedience.

Received the following letter from Ensign Clarke:

"Gentlemen,

" Gentlemen,

" I was this day, to my great surprize, " accosted by one of your servants, who in- " formed me, calling me by name, that the " officers in general were surprized at having " received no letter from me in particular. " I can only say, that the privates in gene- " ral were unwilling to deliver any letter " from me, without seeing the contents. I " might complain of the manner they have " behaved some time since their arrival " here; which has indeed been such, as " shewed they were happy to have it in " their power to insult any one who had " been of a rank superior to themselves with " impunity. However, it is wrong to men- " tion any thing of this kind, as I am at " present in a situation so very disagreeable " in many respects, that any one thing is " scarce worth mentioning, even were it " likely, on my complaints, to be reme- " died.

" I arrived at Madras in January, 1781, " in a style superior to that of the rest of

" the

1781. "the cadets in general, having been two
"years an Enfign and Lieutenant in the
"militia, and of courfe being ufed to a very
"expenfive way of living, together with a
"careleffnefs for money, and lending to too
"many who had no profpect of being able
"to pay me. Notwithftanding this, I
"was largely fupplied by General Munro,
"to whom I was particularly recommend-
"ed, and at whofe houfe I lived at Madras,
"as well as to Mr. Mawbrey, who was
"very much my friend, and two or three
"others. I foon fell into debt to fuch a
"degree, as obliged me to think of going
"to camp, or fome where elfe, in order to
"get out of the reach of the Mayor's
"Court: for which purpofe I applied to
"the Governor, who told me, that as foon
"as a fhip failed for Cuddalore, where our
"army then lay, I might go. But as there
"was danger in waiting fo long, I fet off
"for camp on horfeback, leaving directions
"with a boy, to fend my things as foon as
"poffible. I arrived fafe at Pondicherry,
"where, when at dinner at a French ta-
"vern, I was made prifoner, and that even-
"ing

" ing sent to Meer Saib's, one of Hyder's
" Generals, camp, since killed. Next morn-
" ing, after I arrived at Pondicherry, I was
" offered three hundred rupees per month,
" and again at Meer Saib's camp, if I would
" take service, which I again and again re-
" fused. I staid a short time in the camp
" of Meer Saib, and was afterwards sent
" under a guard of two havaldars and six
" Sepoys to Hyder's camp, then lying near
" Tanjore, commanded by Colonel Braith-
" waite. Two days after my arrival, I was
" taken before the Nabob, who asked me
" the usual questions; to all which I pro-
" fessed ignorance, alledging, that my short
" stay at Madras, and my station, I having
" been appointed Ensign in the 2d battalion
" of 2d regiment, commanded by Major
" Hopkins, prevented my having any in-
" sight into the management of affairs at
" Madras. The next day we marched to
" Trichinopoly, where I understood he was
" to lay for some time. In a few days
" after, good God! what was my surprize,
" to be sent for by the commandant of the
" battalion, with which I was confined,
" and

1781. "and then informed it was Hyder's defire
"that I should embrace Mahomedanism.
"I refused, notwithstanding the most
"dreadful threats, and most alluring pro-
"mises, to consent to a thing so much
"my abhorrence. The next day, my usual
"allowance of rice was brought; but on
"asking for the three pice, my daily pit-
"tance, I was informed it was stopped, till
"I agreed to the proposal of yesterday, of
"becoming a proselyte. I was a little
"shocked, but resolved to persevere, till
"some relief or other should come. On
"the second day after this, I received no
"rice at all, nor the two next days. Be-
"ing now almost worn out, not having
"tasted any food, except a little rice which
"the Sepoys afforded, I with my tongue
"consented to a thing which my heart
"abhorred. On this I received my for-
"mer allowance, and what had been
"stopped the several days foregoing. I
"shortly after marched to Seringapatam,
"in the most horrid despondence of
"mind. On my arrival here, I was
"questioned with regard to my knowledge
"of

" of the exercife, which I faid I knew no-
" thing of: but on the appearance of a
" chaubuc, or horfewhip, I foon went
" through the manual to the fatisfaction of
" the two Myars. I was then queftioned
" with regard to my having confented to
" embrace their damned religion, which I
" denied. However, I was foon, from the
" fecond appearance of the chaubuc and the
" recollection of former ufage, induced to
" fpeak my confent, though on my arri-
" val at the boys you daily fee, and being
" afked if I would teach them your exer-
" cife, I refufed, faying, I had refufed to
" take fervice, or become a Muffulman,
" and that I would rather do both, or even
" die, than teach others to fight againft my
" country, which in my idea was worfe
" than either. I was then removed to the
" prifon where I now am, and found a
" European of the name of Smith, of the
" 2d battalion, 2d regiment, in as miferable
" a fituation as any to which a man could be
" reduced by vermin, dirty cloaths, bed, &c.
" The fecond night after my arrival, I was
" made a Muffulman; about three months
" after

1781. "after my arrival, I was very much sur-
"prised one morning to see a set of young
"men very cleanly dressed, brought for the
"same dreadful operation of which I had
"lately recovered. That night they were
"circumcised after the usual doze of majum
"had been administered: what ensued with
"regard to them you have received from
"them before. I had forgot to mention,
"that at first the usual allowance of mut-
"ton, ghee, &c. was very great, but that
"we had only three cash per day. However,
"on their arrival we had six, and afterwards
"one gold fanam.

"I have done all in my power to prevail
"on them to refuse going to exercise.
"Though I was tied up twice to be flogged,
"I would not go on any account. The
"usage from the privates towards me has
"been most rascally, which, together with
"other things, makes it my daily wish to
"die, and has almost tempted me more
"than once to lay violent hands on myself.
"I hope soon, however, and have very
"good reason to expect, that in a short time
"the

" the arrival of our army will at once put 1781.
" an end to our confinement and Mahome-
" danifm. My having confeffed many things
" againſt myfelf, which otherwife could
" never have appeared, is a fufficient proof
" that I fcorn to palliate any part of my
" offence or mifconduct by a lie.

" I am, my dear brother officers, if my
" folly has not forfeited my right to call
" you by fo dear a name, your affectionate
" fufferer,

"HENRY GEORGE JAMES JENNINGS CLARKE."

Vifited by a head man, or man of confequence from the Durbar, who enquired
very affectionately after our health, and if
we were in want of any thing. He took
his leave with great promifes of friendfhip;
but he executed none.

Received a chit, or note, from Colonel
Baillie, offering us two hundred and fifty
gold fanams.

1781. The cash received from head quarters (so we called Colonel Baillie's prison), when each gentleman received ten fanams.

1782. Jan. 4. Arrived prisoners, three Europeans, with a number of Carnatic children.

5. Fourteen Europeans taken out and circumcised.

6. A Circar Bramin visited us, and in a very peremptory manner ordered us to fall in; and we had reason to suspect he came to single some of us out for his diabolical purpose.

18. Serjeant Higgins, of Captain Powell's battalion, voluntarily took service. This he did with an intention, which he afterwards found means of carrying into effect, to make his escape to his wife, whom he had lately married.

Received a letter from Ensigns Brunton and Gordon, informing us, that they are threatened by the Bramin with being made Musfulmen,

fulmen, and that they intend fome of us 1782.
for the fame purpofe.

Enfigns Brunton and Gordon, with one Jan.
hundred foldiers, removed to Shittle-Droog: 26.
the foldiers hand-cuffed, two and two.

Very much alarmed by the appearance of 27.
a Circar Bramin, who ordered the whole of
us to turn out. His orders being complied
with, he looked ftedfaftly at fix of the ftout-
eft, and then faid to a man who ftood
near him, thefe fix will do. The fix were,
Captains Baird and Wragg; Lieutenants
Lindfey, Bowfer, Coke; and Enfign Macalifter.

Vifited by the Keeladar and Myar. Feb.
3.

Purfa Rama, Colonel Baillie's boy, was 24.
detected in carrying contraband goods to
his mafter; the boy was put in irons and
removed to the foldiers.

A European Muffulman put in the ftocks,
and ftripped naked, for ftriking a caffre,

1782. or black man of the negroe or African kind.

Feb. 26. The European Muſſulman releaſed.

28. A number of Sepoys, who were taken priſoners in a ſally at Trichinopoly, and ſent here, have, on account of their cruel treatment, taken ſervice. The few who have not conſented, are chained two and two, with the daily allowance of one ſear of baggee (a poor ſmall grain), and three caſh.

March 17. Colonel Baillie, Captain Rumley, and Lieutenant Frazer's irons taken off.

18. A corps of Carnatic ſlaves, taken ſince the commencement of the war, and diſ-ciplined by Serjeant Dempſter, with the other European Muſſulmen, marched to join an army to be led againſt Calicut, where we had ſome troops.

Abdiel Wahab (Mahomed-Ally's brother) who was taken priſoner at Chitteput, and ſent priſoner here, allowed for himſelf and

and family, confifting of feventy perfons, 1782. one thoufand rupees per month; his eldeft fon remains at Arcot with Hyder.

Enfign Macauley fent his fhoe buckles to the Keeladar, in order to obtain his leave to difpofe of them, that he might raife a few fanams. The buckles detained by the Keeladar.

Arrived prifoners this evening a number of Europeans, and lodged in a veranda near our prifon. Their number, rank, and the place where they were taken, we have not been able to learn. March 26.

Vifited by the Myar, who, after reconnoitring our prifon, ordered the cook-room to be cleaned out, for the unfortunate people who arrived yefterday. We hear the found of the armourers employed in putting on their irons. Various are our conjectures where they have been taken. However, we at prefent flatter ourfelves that they may only be the officers feparated from us in Hyder's camp, and fent to Bangalore. 27.

1782. Two of our servants removed to Colonel Baillie. A letter sent to the soldiers.

Abdiel Wahab sent us word, that Hyder meant to force Colonel Baillie, and the rest of the officers, to enter into his service.

The prisoners that had been lodged in the veranda were brought in here this evening: Seventeen European officers, one surgeon, and one black commandant. They are the officers of Colonel Braithwaite's detachment, and fell into the hands of Tippoo Saib, in the Tanjore country, the 18th of February, 1782, about forty miles from Tanjore. During the time they were with Tippoo Saib, he paid them every attention that was necessary. He not only furnished them with cloaths and money, but at the same time gave strict orders to all his Keeladars to be attentive to them during their march to Hyder's camp, who was then lying at Conjeveram. But on their arrival at this place, their money, and every other little thing they had, was taken from them; and they were told, that if they concealed the most trifling

trifling article, their nose and ears would be cut off. The next day, a few piah horses were provided for their journey; but many of them were obliged to walk the whole way, with the daily allowance of six or seven sears of rice, with a little salt, amongst the whole. Colonel Braithwaite and Ensign Holmes remain in Hyder's camp. We are informed that our army is lying near Madras, for want of carriage bullocks, and that it was believed a French fleet had passed Pulicat.

These circumstances aggravated the melancholy gloom that had long hung over the place of our confinement.

The following is a list of the killed and wounded of Colonel Braithwaite's detachment, taken by Tippoo Saib, on the 18th of February, 1782.

Names.	Killed.	Wounded
Colonel Braithwaite		1
Captain Judson		
Lieut. Lind .		
Carry over		1

Lieut.

1782.

Names.	Killed.	Wounded.
Brought over		1
Lieut. Eastland		
Gillon		1
Sampson		1
Cameron		1
Ensign Graham		1
Loy		1
Gahagan		
Kennet		1
Macauley		
Thewlis		1
Fenwick		
Holmes		1
Haywood		1
Stewart	1	
Mr. White, surgeon		
Lieut. Bowles }		
Latcliff } Nabob's Service		1
Clowman }		
	1	11

April 9. Captain Baird's irons taken off, on account of sickness.

Arrived prisoner, one European officer; but no further account.

Lieu-

Lieutenant Lind, at the point of death, is 1782. allowed, with the utmoſt difficulty, to have April 10. his irons taken off.

Lieutenant Coke's irons were taken off, 12. by the means of a bribe to the Verduvalla, a military officer non-commiſſioned, about the rank of a ſerjeant-major.

Lieutenant Lind died.   14.

The dead body of Lieutenant Lind, 15. laſhed to a bamboo, was carried out on the ſhoulders of three men. We all of us ſtood around the body of our departed friend, while Mr. Skardon read the funeral ſervice.

Viſited by the Myar, who enquired in a May moſt preſſing manner, if there were any car- 9. penters or ſmiths amongſt us. We replied, that we were all gentlemen. He did not ſeem ſatisfied with this anſwer; but deſired the Commandant, Sid Abrim, to make particular enquiry, and inform him the next viſit

1782. visit he should make, as the Keeladar meant to take some of us out.

May 15.
An order arrives from Hyder for our servants to discontinue going to the Buzar. Henceforth our guards are our market-men, who cheat us most unmercifully.

31.
Ensign Graham's irons taken off, on account of sickness.

June 4.
In honour of his Majesty's birth-day, we have celebrated it with a pilaw, and drank his health in sherbet.

17.
Visited by the Myar. He enquired for a cavalry officer of the name of Galeet, who, he said, belonged to Colonel Baillie's detachment. There was no such person.

19.
Arrived prisoners, fourteen European children, eight boys and six girls. It is reported that they were taken at Cuddalore.

22.
Mr. Hope's irons taken off, on account of sickness.

Captain

Captain Lucas and Enſign Maconichy's irons taken off, on account of ſickneſs. 1782. June 28.

Lieutenant Gillon, and Enſigns Thewlis and Latcliff are put in irons.

Repeated applications have been made to the Keeladar for medicine, and for the French Doctor to attend thoſe gentlemen who are at preſent in a dangerous way: but the cruel tyrant will neither order nor allow the ſmalleſt aſſiſtance. Thoſe who are fortunate enough to enjoy a good ſtate of health attend the ſick in the night. 29.

At half paſt eight, P. M. died Captain Lucas, brother to the celebrated patriot of that name in England. The Captain's death was bitterly lamented by the whole priſon. He was diſtinguiſhed by good natural talents as well as acquired accompliſhments. In his manners he was unaſſuming, amiable, and engaging : and the cheerfulneſs and vivacity of his temper, which were expreſſed in lively ſongs and facetious ſallies, July 5.

ſcattered

scattered frequent rays of mirth on our gloomy mansion.

July 7.

At three o'clock, A. M. died Mr. Hope, a Cadet in the Company's service.

9.

About twelve, A. M. died Ensign Maconichy.

As Mr. White, Colonel Braithwaite's surgeon, was unacquainted with the simples and compositions used as medicines in this country, and was deprived of his own chest of medicines, the arrival of that gentleman amongst us, (against whose professional abilities this ought not certainly to be consiered, and is not intended, as any insinuation) in the character of a fellow-prisoner, did not avail us. We therefore continued to be our own physicians, and to use those medicines with whose powers several of us had become acquained in the course of a long residence, in various stations and situations in India. The natives of this country, in which nature is very powerful and luxuriant,

luxuriant, and where maxims and obfervations are accumulated and handed down from generation to generation, from very remote antiquity, are undoubtedly acquainted with many medicinal properties of herbs and fruits, and other fimples, unknown to European nations. It is generally known, that the practice of inoculating for the fmallpox is common in all Afiatic countries. But there is an art in Hindoftan, not yet known in Europe, by which the women effectually prevent all traces of the fmallpox on the faces of their little ones. This prefervative is compofed of a falve made of certain Indian herbs, and a certain kind of oil, which they apply the moment the pock begins to blacken. It does not appear, that any of the Company's furgeons have ever enquired, or at leaft enquired with fuccefs, into the nature of this preparation. That the Hindoos, however, know how to fave their fkins from the ravages of the fmallpox, is a fact which cannot be doubted. On the fubject of Hindoo furgery and phyfic, another well-attefted fact may be mentioned, which is attended with the happieft effects.

1782.

1782. effects. When any person happens to receive a bruise or wound in any part of his body, by a fall or blow, or otherwise, those who are nearest to him, presently strip off the greater part of his cloaths, and, with the palms of their hands, gently rub the afflicted part, or if that is not to be touched, the parts nearest to it; and proceeding from that spot, rub over, with greater force, the whole of the body. This good office is generally performed by the women, who are indeed the surgeons and physicians of this country, and who handle their patients with all the easy address of the most experienced member of the faculty in Europe.

It was from the natives of India, that the English, at Madras, learned the qualities of the junglicarandee, or what are commonly called by our soldiers Jack Spratt's Nuts, three of which will operate as an emetic, with very salutary effects. Cassia, jaggeree, and tamarinds, were the *Materia Medica* of our cathartics. These materials, with some quicksilver, which we formed into pills and ointments, we were obliged to introduce by

stealth,

stealth, by means of handsome rewards to individuals belonging to our guards; for, as has already been observed, all medicines were prohibited by the Keeladar, under the severest threats.

1782.

Arrived prisoners, five hundred Carnatic boys, in order to be made slaves, and to be entered into Hyder's slave battalions. We hear the French have taken some of our ships, and given up the prisoners to Hyder.

July 13.

Arrived prisoners, two Europeans.

24.

Lieutenant Sampson put in irons.

26.

A chit, or note, is received from Colonel Baillie, requesting some mercurial pills. He says, they have not the smallest idea, why their irons were taken off. The pills sent.

Arrived prisoners, three European officers, as also a mate of a country ship.

30.

One

1782.
Aug. 10.
One of our officers struck by a centinel, for attempting to look out at the prison door.

13. Lieutenant Coke and Ensign Graham put in irons.

Lieutenant Lindsey's irons taken off, on account of sickness.

The French, we hear from every quarter, have made over three hundred seamen, and others, whom they had taken prisoners, to Hyder; and that the French Admiral received from Hyder, on that account, fifty thousand rupees. This was publicly affirmed at the Keeladar's Durbar; but it is given merely as a report.

Sept. 22.
We are informed that Colonel Baillie is in a dangerous way; yet that the Keeladar will not allow him a physician to attend him, nor even assist him with medicines, although many applications have been made to him for that purpose.

Arrived

Arrived prisoners, three hundred Carnatic boys.   1782.

The whole of us have offered one hundred and twenty thousand rupees for our enlargement; and not to serve against Hyder during the war. No answer.   Oct. 13.

Arrived prisoners, seven Europeans.   18.

A letter taken charge of by one of our guard, to the soldiers prison, with a promise, if an answer is received by us, to give him three pagodas. Subscribed one fanam each for that purpose.   26.

Arrived forty Europeans; part of those men that were given up by the French. They have been circumcised.   30.

Arrived prisoners, eight hundred Carnatic boys and girls.   Nov. 2.

A Sepoy has undertaken to carry a letter to the circumcised Europeans.   10.

Vol. II.   F   Received

1782.
Nov.
13.
Received the melancholy news of Colonel Baillie's death.

This melancholy event excited painful reflections on the uncertainty of prosperity and of fame, both of which are greatly under the controul of fortune. Colonel Baillie possessed great vigour both of body and mind, being of a middling stature, well and firmly made, and animated on all occasions with calm and steady resolution. Before the unfortunate day that consigned him to a confinement, from which he was destined never to escape, he uniformly bore the character of an officer enterprizing, brave, and judicious. As his merit and rank had rendered him an object of terror to the conqueror before he fell into his hands, so he became an object of barbarous resentment afterwards, and was treated, accordingly, with unusual and marked severity. In the enemy's camp, he was separated from his fellow prisoners, the Captains Rumley and Frazer, and thrown into irons even on his journey to Seringapatam from Arcot. On his arrival on his way to the capital of Hyder,

Hyder, at Bangalore, five guns were fired in 1781. order to affemble the people to infult his misfortunes. And during the whole courfe of his illnefs, he received not the leaft comfort or affiftance from the advice of any phyfician.

Arrived prifoners, one European, with three hundred Carnatic boys.

Received the following from Lieutenants Speediman and Rutlidge.

"We were yefterday agreeably furprifed
" by receiving a letter from you, which has
" been our conftant wifh fince we have
" been here, and are extremely obliged to
" you for the trouble you undoubtedly muft
" have had in forwarding it, having made
" many attempts of that kind ourfelves, but
" never could fucceed—but particularly for
" the concern you feel on our account, and
" the promifes you make us of reprefenting
" our fituation to thofe in whofe power
" it will be to extricate us out of this af-
" flicting fituation.

F 2   " You

1782. "You have requested us to relate to you
"the particulars of our ill fortune, and
"also to answer some questions, which
"you have set down, both of which we
"will readily comply with, as far as lies in
"our power. We are sorry we cannot give
"you as satisfactory an account as pro-
"bably you might expect, being wounded
"in January last, and left in Vellore: but
"what news we send is what we got
"from Ensign Byrne, who came up to
"Vellore in June, with one company of
"Sepoys, three three-pounders, and a
"good many Polygars, with provisions for
"the garrison; and we, being anxious to
"join the army, left Vellore to go back
"with him: but we had not quitted the
"place above eighteen hours, when Tippoo
"Saib's whole force came down upon us.
"We fought them for some time: then
"the Polygars left the Company's troops
"in a mob, with what intention God
"knows; but Tippoo's troops cut in among
"them. What escaped the sword were
"made prisoners. In this situation, desert-
"ed by those people, most of our Sepoys
"being

" being wounded, and our ammunition
" nearly expended, we hoifted a white
" handkerchief for quarter, which they
" granted immediately, and we were made
" prifoners by a French officer. Byrne was
" made prifoner by a black Commandant.
" While we remained in Tippoo's camp,
" we were very well ufed; but when we
" arrived at his father's we had reafon to re-
" pent the exchange, receiving only a mea-
" fure of rice and one pice a day. We how-
" ever continued with him five days, the
" laft of which in the evening we were fent
" for by Hyder's Dewan, who ordered Mr.
" Byrne only in irons, but both of us to be
" put in with a parcel of fmall boys, along
" with whom we found Serjeant-major
" Groves, of Colonel Braithwaite's detach-
" ment. Next morning, about two o'clock,
" we marched for Seringapatam. After
" four or five day's march we were overta-
" ken by Byrne, and Lieutenant Crewitzer
" of the Cavalry, who, with a troop belong-
" ing to the grand guard near Arneé, were
" cut off, which is probably what has been
" reprefented to you as a regiment of ca-
"   valry,

1782. "valry, there having been no other accident
"of the kind. We were a good deal fur-
"prifed to find that Byrne and we were
"bound for different places; but never
"gueffed their horrid intentions with re-
"gard to us, until our arrival at Seringapa-
"tam, when, inftead of being put amongft
"you, we were marched with the boys in-
"to a large fquare building, about a mile
"eaftward of the Fort, in the new village
"of Gunjam Pett, where we found nine
"Europeans, and were rendered almoft
"fpeechlefs when they told us, that they
"were all made Muffulmen againft their
"inclinations, and that it was moft pro-
"bable we fhould fhare the fame fate:
"we now found ourfelves in a moft mifer-
"able fituation, as different parties, from
"the guard that was over us, were coming
"every hour of the day, fometimes making
"great promifes if we would confent to be
"circumcifed; and, at others, with drawn
"fwords, chaubucks, and ropes ready to
"tie us; the barber in the rear ready to
"fhave our heads. This method they con-
"tinued feven or eight days; but finding
"both

"both their threats and promises equally 1782.
"ineffectual, they took another method to
"make us consent, by separating us, and
"allowing no one to speak to us. But
"finding that this method had as little ef-
"fect as the others, the Jemmidar took
"compassion on us, and wrote to Hyder in
"our behalf. During the time we waited
"for an answer, we imagined they had
"dropt their infamous intentions, and daily
"expected to be sent to you. This inter-
"val of hope, however, proved to be but a
"dream, which was effectually broken on the
"27th of August, by the appearance of ten
"or twelve stout fellows, with chaubucks
"in their hands, and as many caffres with
"ropes to tie us with. They made no cere-
"mony, but seized, tied us, cut off our
"hair, and then walked away, like villains
"that had been bred up to such business,
"and left us to lament our hard fate.

"The same villains again made their ap- Sept.
"pearance, seized and tied us as before, 1.
"and stood over us while they obliged us
"to eat a sort of stuff called majum, which
"nearly

1782. "nearly divested us of our senses, and,
" in the same evening, they accomplished
" their vile design. During the time we
" were with them, we would take nothing
" from them but rice, nor would we per-
" mit them to take off our irons, which
" they often offered to do, least they should
" imagine that we were contented with our
" situation. We receive a gold fanam a
" day, and are obliged to drill a number of
" boys sent from the Carnatic to be circum-
" cised, and kept in these squares. Thank
" God, what they know will never do the
" Company any harm.

Received the 18th
 Nov. 1782.
(Signed.)
" JAMES SPEEDIMAN,
" RICHARD RUTLIDGE."

Received the following letter from Serjeant Dempster:

" Gentlemen,

" Your notes I received. Messrs. Speedi-
" man and Rutlidge have so fully answer-
" ed

" ed your feveral queftions, concerning the 1782.
" prefent war fubfifting between the Com-
" pany and Hyder, that any thing that I
" could add would be no more than mere
" repetition. If I don't miftake, however, they
" have omitted to make mention of anything
" appertaining to a peace. Such a thing is
" not talked of; and from what I have col-
" lected from a ferjeant who arrived here
" a few days ago, who has fhared the fate
" common to the reft of us here, it feems,
" that things don't wear any tolerable com-
" plexion, all owing to the arrival of the
" French."

Received the following lift of captives from the midfhipmen taken by Monfieur Suffrein, and given up to Hyder-Ally-Cawn:

" Hannibal, of 50 guns, February 14,
" 1782. Meffrs. Lefage, Auftin, and Drake,
" midfhipmen.

" The Chacer, of 18 guns, February
" 14. No officer here.
" The

1782.
"The Rake transport, June 6, off the
"Cape, Mr. Wilkinson, midshipman.

"The Resolution, June 9, Mr. Hidde-
"man, Master's mate.

"The Yarmouth and Fortitude, Com-
"pany's ships, June 27. No officer.

"The number of men belonging to all
"the ships here are forty-four, and officers
"belonging to the King's service, five.—
"In February, the French fleet came on
"the coast, consisting of twelve sail of the
"line; and the English of nine. They
"had an action the 17th of February,
"which lasted three hours and an half; and
"on the 12th of April, the English, of
"eleven sail, and the French of twelve,
"engaged near Trincomally for five hours
"and a half; the French much damaged:
"and, on the 28th of June, they engaged
"off Cuddalore, with the same ships as be-
"fore, for two hours: one French sixty-
"four struck, but she was covered by her
"own ships; another sixty-four dismasted.
"The

" The English have drove the French off
" the coast.

" On the 30th of June the French sent
" all the prisoners ashore at Cuddalore, and
" delivered them into the hands of Hyder,
" and marched us into Chillumbrum.—
" The 12th of August they marched us to
" Bangalore; on the 20th of October they
" picked out all the youngest of the men
" and officers, and marched us to Seringa-
" patam; and, on the 7th of November,
" they shaved our heads, and on the 10th
" they made us Mussulmen. Since we have
" been here they have given us some dun-
" geree, or coarse cloth, and mats to sleep
" on.

" The 7th of November the Myar came
" to us just before they shaved our heads,
" and told us that we were never to be re-
" leased, but to be kept here, and to be as
" the Nabob's sons, which makes us very
" unhappy, thinking we shall never see our
" native country any more; but when you
" are exchanged, we hope that you will
" make

1782. "make our case known to our fellow-sub-
"jects. We are all exceedingly sorry to
"hear of Colonel Baillie's death. Mr.
"Austin would be glad to hear from you,
"if it is agreeable. We have here amongst
"the sufferers,

  Messrs. LESAGE,
    WILKINSON,
    AUSTIN, } Midshipmen.
    DRAKE,
    HEIDEMAN,

Lieutenant Massey and Doctor White's irons taken off, on account of sickness.

Nov. 1. Account of a treaty of peace being on foot in the Carnatic, but on account of the arrival of some French troops, with the King of France's picture (for Hyder), it was broken off.

Received the following journal from Serjeant Dempster, which had been sent to him from some of the unfortunate Europeans, dated March 14, 1782.

         "Assembled

" Affembled at Seringapatam, under the 1782.
" command of Buffadar Cawn, Jemmidar,
" who received the chaylacks (Carnatic boys
" circumcifed and made flaves) from Seati-
" bie Jemmidar, befide the chaylack battalion,
" twelve hundred horfe, three battalions of
" Sepoys, with firelocks, of about five hun-
" dred men, eight gunners, twelve Lafcars,
" four rocket-boys, one man with a bow
" and arrows, three thoufand feven hundred
" and feventy-five Polygars with pikes,
" match-locks, &c.: total, five thoufand,
" and our artillery park, of four three
" pounders, iron. When our camp is pitch-
" ed, 'tis all of a clufter, about twenty
" tents, an old marqui, and one thoufand
" huts.

" Agreeably to Seatibie's orders, our vic-
" tuals was cooked with the Commandant's
" and Subadar's. However, they foon fhook
" off that incumbrance, and put us on
" the footing of the flave boys. This even-
" ing they had taken the currey pot away,
" and we had been waiting for it a confider-
" able time: but they not ferving them-
" felves,

" selves, Green and Woodley seized it, and
" ran off with it, and we served ourselves, to
" the great mortification of the Comman-
" dant, Subadars, and Myars, who swore
" they would be revenged on all the ferin-
" gees next day.

" 15. Marched to Mysore; the old Com-
" mandant, agreeably to his vow of revenge
" of yesterday, orders the slave-boys rice to
" be cooked for us: but we all refused it,
" Higgins excepted. The Commandant
" went to the Jemmidar and informed him that
" we had been drinking arrack: whereupon
" we were made prisoners, two and two,
" and put under centinels of an out batta-
" lion, our swords being taken from us.—
" About midnight they sent us some good
" rice. The next day they released us, and
" gave us back our swords. An order issued
" to deter us from buying arrack and
" toddy.

" 17. Arrived at a fort where we receiv-
" ed a reinforcement of one thousand Poly-
" gars

" gars from Shittle-Droog: halted three
" days and left two guns behind us.

" 22. Entered into very thick woods.—
" After marching eight miles within the
" woods, the Polygars in front were furpri-
" fed by about eighty of the enemy, the
" Niars, by the Moors called Nimars, a fet
" of people formerly fubdued by Hyder,
" but now in a ftate of rebellion: of this
" caft is our Commandant and two of our
" Subadars. They difcharged a few match-
" locks and arrows at the Polygars, who
" came running back with their ufual bra-
" very. However, they were beat back
" again to the attack with large bamboos
" and clubs, by the Verduvalla belonging to
" the chaylacks. On this a fmall fkirmifh
" enfued; and as the chaylacks advanced,
" the Englifh drum beat, which caufed the
" enemy to retreat to the woods. Seven of
" the enemy were taken, one of whom was
" hanged on a tree, and ten killed. Halt-
" ed at this place two days.

" 25.

1782. "25. Marched near twelve miles, and came upon about three hundred of the enemy; a skirmish of about a quarter of an hour happened, in which five of them were killed and four taken. We had three killed and wounded. The enemy set off to the woods.

"26. In our march took three Niars, who gave information of the enemy being posted in a large village to the right.— Upon our arrival there, we found that the enemy had fled. An alarm happened here about midnight: it was a false one: however, our troops were very much frightened.

"27. The Niars taken yesterday were hanged.

"The Europeans were put under centinels to their companies, on which account we refused doing duty, and gave up our swords; for which Higgins was bound with his hands behind him all day.— Smith, Innwood, and Clements, beat with
"rattans,

" rattans, and in the evening after we en-
" camped, we were all tied in one rope, and
" ordered to be beat: however, we received
" our fwords and were releafed.

" 28. Arrived at a fmall mud fort in
" which were three hundred of the enemy.
" They fired a few ginjauls, a long kind of
" guns made of bar iron bound by hoops,
" of which they had twenty, at our mob:
" and early in the morning they quitted the
" fort and efcaped. At day-light our peo-
" ple entered it: halted here twenty days:
" parties fent out daily, and brought in
" prifoners, fome of whom were hanged,
" others difcharged after paying a fine of
" their nofes, ears, or left hands.

" April 4. About five hundred of the
" enemy in fight. The troops being formed
" for battle, and the enemy amongft the
" bufhes in front, they fired at them from
" the three-pounders, and afterwards advan-
" ced, and platooned with fmall arms. The
" enemy fired pretty warmly feveral times,
" but being clofe purfued by our mob, they

Vol. II. G " made

1782. "made off to the woods; how many were
"killed of them is unknown. Nine heads
"brought in to the Jemmidars. Thus
"ended the affair with the Niars for this
"time.

"April 18. We marched out of this
"woody country, and, on the twenty-firſt,
"arrived at a fort called Goondull.——
"N. B. Greens, an old Subadar, was convict-
"ed before the Jemmidar of endeavouring to
"perſuade the chaylacks to leave the guns,
"and go to the Niars, being one himſelf;
"he was tied to a poſt, and reduced to a
"private Sepoy, but is excuſed all duty
"by his brother Niar the old Comman-
"dant.—

"23. Arrived at the fort we had left on
"the twenty-third of March. The Jem-
"midar ordered a Sepoy to be beat in a
"barbarous manner by four men with large
"bamboos, and then to be dragged round
"the camp, on his belly, by ſix men, for
"cutting his wife with his ſword in two or
"three places.

"24.

" 24. Arrived at a fort called Perripatam, 1782,
" and halted five days.

" May 1. Marched to a village called
" Citty Pore, near which was the ruins of
" a small fort, which had been poffeffed by
" the Corakees, a fet of people formerly
" fubdued, but who had afterwards rebelled,
" deftroyed the fort and fled. The country
" here is woody, and the Niar country dif-
" tant from Perripatam twenty miles.

" 2. Arrived on a plain, where a Cora-
" kee Rajah joined our mob, with three
" hundred of his men, armed with match-
" locks and broad knives: proceeded on till
" we came to a small fort built with large
" timber, in which were two hundred and
" fifty Corakees: fome of our troops were
" detached with three companies of chay-
" lacks to fire mufquetry at it under cover of
" a high bank, which was not of the leaft
" fervice; the other chaylack company ftaid
" in the rear for a body guard to the Com-
" mande in chief. The enemy behaved ob-
" ftinately and refolutely. Although they had
" no

1782. "no guns, they fired very hot from their
"ginjauls and match-locks, of which our
"three-pound balls scarcely pierced the tim-
"ber. At night we drew off to encamp, after
"firing about eight thousand musquet balls.
"During the night the enemy left the fort,
"and did not lose a man in their retreat,
"and at ten o'clock in the morning, the
"place was entered by the four companies
"of Sepoys. Thus ended the Corakee affair
"at present. Within sixteen miles of this
"fort, are near twenty Corakees hanging
"on trees for their late insurrection. The
"Carokee Rajah and his men sent to Citty
"Pore to settle there, for their loyalty.—
"This is the most cowardly mob that was
"ever known, from the Commander in
"chief to the wild Polygars: on the line of
"march we were like a flock of sheep.

"6. Arrived at a stone fort called Mar-
"carry, where several Bramins had been de-
"frauding the troops, who made their com-
"plaint to the Jemmidar, who ordered a cock
"of a firelock to be fixed upon their ears,
"and made them stand upon one foot, till
"they

"they agreed to make good the damage fuf-
"tained by the troops of the town, through
"their villainy. At this place, are feven
"companies of Sepoys with mufquets,
"lately came from Nagram, and a Portu-
"gueze captain who commands thirty
"mufteer artillery men. Halted here eight
"days. The monfoons and rainy feafon
"fetting in. The mob ordered to canton
"at Perripatam till orders from the Nabob,
"where a ftabula was to be built for the
"chaylack battalion; what will be the
"next exploit God knows, but neither
"Niars nor Corakees are fettled yet. After
"fteering all points of the compafs, we are
"about forty miles from you: this is a
"moft plentiful country.

1782.

"Auguft 21. Intelligence came to the
"Jemmidar that a large body of the Co-
"rakees were affembling near Marcarry:
"three thoufand Polygars were detached
"from Perripatam cantonement, and three
"hundred Sepoys from Marcarry; they
"came up with the enemy near a large
"river; they fkirmifhed for above three
"quarters

1782. "quarters of an hour, when the Corakees
"charged the Polygars. The whole of our
"party were defeated: only fifty Sepoys ef-
"caped.

"Sept. 23. A harcarrah came with in-
"telligence, that the Corakees had made an
"attempt upon Citty Pore, with an inten-
"tion of putting to death the Rajah and
"his men. The Jemmidar marched with
"his mob of about four thousand cow-
"ards, to Sickle Boor, six miles, and en-
"camped.

"27 and 28. Continually skirmished
"by the enemy, who often surprized our
"mob by springing out of the jungle or
"wood. In the evening of the twenty-
"eight arrived at Citty Pore; relieved the
"fort by leaving two hundred and fifty Se-
"poys in the room of the Rajah and his
"men received in camp; our loss before we
"arrived here thirty men.

"29. Marched from hence; on our way
"back skirmished; lost fourteen men and
"encamped

" encamped at Sickle Boor that evening: 1782.
" all but fifty of the men belonging to the
" Corakee Rajah deferted us.

" 30. In the evening, the enemy very
" near our camp. The Jemmidar ordered the
" mufic belonging to the match-locks, the
" infantry drums, and cavalry trumpets, to
" be beat and founded all round the camp
" every gurry (twenty-three minutes) du-
" ring the night, in order to frighten away
" the enemy.

" Oct. 2. Marched about ten miles, and
" found the roads ftopped with large trees
" laid acrofs; during the time the labourers
" were clearing them away, the enemy
" fired very hot, both fides of the road, and
" put our negroes to the rout, and took all
" our buzar and baggage. Several fkir-
" mifhes happened on our way to Citty
" Pore, in which we had one European,
" upwards of one hundred blacks, killed;
" and three Europeans fixty blacks wound-
" ed. In great confufion we arrived at
" Citty Pore that evening, where we re-
" mained

1782. "mained five days; during which time a treaty of peace was concluded between the Jemmidar and the Corakee prince.

"Sept. 8. Our mob was efcorted by three thoufand fix hundred Corakees on each flank within five miles of Perripatam: it was unadoubtedly great folly of the Corakee Prince to let us come off fo eafily, as they muft have cut us off entirely.

"The fort of Citty Pore was given over to them, as well as all other pretentions to their country.

"On the eighteenth of October two thoufand men joined us from Seringapatam."

Here ends the Journal tranfmitted to us by Serjeant Dempfter.

The following was sent from Bentall 1782. Woodley to Serjeant Dempster.

" Dear D.
" I assure you our situation is very bad,
" much worse than yours. The old Com-
" mandant draws five pagodas per month;
" but our pay and the Subadar's is only one
" fanam a day, which changes only for
" eight pice and three cash. The Verdu-
" valla serjeant draws three-fourths of a fa-
" nam a-day, the Verduvalla corporal one
" pice, one cash, the Havaldar half a fanam, a
" Sepoy one fourth of a fanam per day, and
" the provisions that are cooked for the Eu-
" ropeans and boys are all on an equality.
" The Commandant and Subadars eat (like
" gentlemen) by themselves; but we like
" slaves, have rice, boiled twice a-day in a
" dirty poisonous manner, with a little cur-
" ry made with doll only. Five seer of
" ghee per day for five hundred men. We
" have not had any meat but twice these
" two months past, on which account it
" costs us all our eight dubs and three cash
" per day for victuals. We are treated ill
" by the old Commandant, who has full
" com-

1782. "command of the battalion; for we have
"no command, only at exercise. The Jem-
"midar, commander in chief, who hates all
"Europeans, answers all our complaints
"with jow, jow! (go, go!)

"Mackinnon, being wounded at the Co-
"rakee fort through the arm with a musket
"ball by one of our own mob, the Jemmi-
"dar made him a present of a red turban
"and a set of gold beads, value ten pago-
"das: all the boys that were wounded re-
"ceived a present of silver bangles to wear
"on their wrists, value twenty-six rupees.
"On the 25th of June, Smithey, Green,
"Clements, Anderson, Wyllies, Mackenzie,
"and your humble servant, endeavoured to
"venture towards Calicut, with a determi-
"nation to extricate ourselves out of Hy-
"der's service. After walking by the light
"of the moon near six cofs, through the
"thickest woods, we were surprized by wild
"elephants and tygers, and by accident lost
"our bread, which determined us to
"turn back again, which we accordingly
"did; and it seems Higgins, being afraid
"he

" he should be brought into trouble, re-
" ported us gone to Seringapatam, to com-
" plain of the Jemmidar's usage. The
" horse being sent out after us, met us about
" five miles from the cantonement, and
" brought us to the Jemmidar. We said,
" by way of excuse, that we had been out
" a-shooting, having a carabine and two
" pistols with us: we were stripped and all
" tied in one rope: an hundred of the stout-
" est of our own battalion received each a
" twig of a tamarind tree and served us out
" a lash each: we had no centinels over us
" before we began this adventure, but now
" we are closely guarded.

1782.

(Signed)
" BENTALL WOODLEY."

Tippoo Saib and Lally on their march to the Malabar coast.

Nov. 2.

Arrived prisoners, two Europeans with fifty Carnatic boys.

Recived

1782.
Nov. 25.
Received a letter from the foldiers, and gave the Sepoy who brought it five fanams.

Dec. 11.
Forty-feven feamen, who were given up to Hyder by Suffrein, appeared this morning on the parade oppofite to our prifon, and have been circumcifed fince their arrival here: they were in the Mahomedan drefs, white turbans, white linen jackets and long drawers; fixteen of thefe unfortunate victims could not be above twelve or thirteen years of age.

A European Muffulman in irons.

Arrived prifoner, one European.

Dec. 12.
The European Muffulman who was put in irons yefterday, is this evening attending the drill in irons.

15.
Received accounts of Hyder's death, and that his corpfe was carried to Collard.—
He

He died of an ulcer in his back, which had afflicted him for seven years.

1782.

Copy of a letter sent to Serjeant Dempster.

" The gentlemen confined in this prison,
" return you their sincere thanks for your
" attention to their last request, and assure
" you, that should it ever hereafter be in their
" power to be of service to you, they shall
" not be unmindful of the favours they have
" received from you in their present unfortu-
" nate situation. Your readiness to oblige us
" in the last instance, leads us to make another
" request to you of the most serious conse-
" quence to us, and which we think can
" be attended with no danger to you, or
" detriment to the service you are unluckily
" fallen into. It is to forward to some Eng-
" lish or neutral settlement, on either coast,
" a small letter which we shall entrust to
" you open, and which will only contain a
" state of the prison and the names of those
" at present living, with a request of tranf-
" mitting the same to Madras. To you,
" who

1782. "who know the length of time we have
"been shut up from all communication
"with our friends, we need not point out
"the advantages we may derive, and the
"satisfaction they must feel, from receiving
"some account of us; or, on the other
"hand, the many fatal events that may
"take place from a supposition of our death.
"Though an opportunity to comply with
"this proposal may not at present offer, yet
"you may keep the letter by you, and,
"from the many detachments and escorts
"that leave this place, one must occur in
"course of time.

"We could therefore wish (if you come
"into our plan) to send you our letter by
"the hand that conveys this. Whatever
"reward you may think necessary, we will
"engage to have paid at Madras, or other
"of our forts, and think we can promise
"the same, should the letter be delivered at
"a neutral settlement; we request therefore
"that you will be so kind as to deliver the
"accompanying letter to Messrs. Speediman
"and

" and Rutlidge, and thank you for the per- 1782.
" ufal of Woodley's Journal.

" If you have any communication with
" Monſ. Fortuno, the French furgeon, we
" requeſt that you will endeavour to fend us
" a few dozens of Tartar Emetic, and a liſt
" of country medicines, to be purchafed in
" the Buzar. When you wiſh to anſwer
" this, or at any other time to write to us,
" let the fignal be, the putting a handker-
" chief over your turban, whilſt at drill on
" the parade.

Tippoo and Lally on their return to Dec.
the Carnatic, in confequence of Hyder's 16.
death.

Arrived a new Keeladar (Nabbee Cawn) 21.
with one battalion of Sepoys, muſtered by
the head Myar and an Arab.

Muſtered by a Circar Bramin, who took 27.
our names, with corps, and rank of each.

Received

1782. Received the following letter from Captain Rumley and Lieutenant Frazer.

"The poor Colonel (meaning Baillie)
"had been ill for some months before he
"died, and I think would have recovered,
"if he had had any assistance, but the
"cruel rascals would not admit of Doctor
"White or the Frenchman coming near
"him, although they saw his sufferings were
"beyond description: we got a sort of coffin
"made for him, and some Sepoys, Peons,
"and a European attended his funeral. We
"are beset by eleven guards, ten golaks, one
"Commandant, Subadar, Myar, and Ver-
"duvalla, and allowed a quarter of damna-
"ble goat, a measure and half of rice, a
"little milk, three loaves of bread each,
"about the size of a six pound shot, some
"ghee, curry stuff, wood, and six cash per
"day between us. They will not let us
"have a knife to cut a bit of cloth, nor the
"sight of a book; so you see we are pret-
"tily situated."

Hyder's

Hyder's death made public at the Cut- 1782. cheree, and the naggars (large drums beat every day at twelve in the great fquare) ordered to difcontinue beating for three days, on account of that event.

Received the following letter from Serjeant Dempfter: a fubfcription of two dubs each, to requite the Sepoy who brought it.

" Gentlemen,
" Your note of the 15th December I
" received: the fhort but real picture of
" your very unfortunate fituation has made
" me melt into tears of fympathy, that
" our name and our country fhould thus
" be the fport of barbarians; and be-
" lieve me, gentlemen, that there is no-
" thing within the verge of my power
" that could alleviate in the fmalleft de-
" gree your prefent fufferings, in the great
" anxiety you muft be in to hear fome
" folacing account after fo long an interval
" of fufpence and confinement, that would
" not moft readily be embraced.—I am ex-
" ceedingly forry that it is not at prefent in
" my

1782. "my power to give you any full or satis-
"factory account. The grand news is as
"follows: That on the 29th of November
"departed this life Hyder-Ally-Cawn: he
"is succeeded by his eldest son Tippoo Saib,
"who bears a very good character indeed;
"he is now at the grand camp near Vel-
"lore. In consequence of the above, about
"fifteen days ago arrived here a new Keela-
"dar: he acts conjunctly with the old one,
"as *very* a villain as exists.

"I could gather no more from the ser-
"jeant, than that he was taken some months
"ago near Trincomally with two hundred
"Sepoys. No juncture of time so barren
"of news as the present, chiefly owing to
"the death of Hyder: every one's mouth
"is full of it. You do me a great deal of
"honour in confiding a trust in me to for-
"ward your letter to the Carnatic, and be
"fully assured that no means or opportunity
"shall be omitted. I sincerely thank you
"for your favour, and promise of protection
"hereafter. I never intend to avail myself
"of it, as the title of Deserter is almost in-
            "supportable

supportable to any one tinctured with the smallest atom of spirit. From the most robust as well as healthy constitution, I am totally changed into a habit that daily tells me my stay shall not be long. Then be expeditious in sending your letter.— This revolution offers a field for much news. Tokens as usual. Sorry I am that I can't add any thing else. This I have writ only with the light of the fire; otherwise the seeing me occupied with pen and ink would subject me to be examined.— As this town is now full of spies, poor Mr. Clarke has been sent to camp about two months ago, to fill the place of a Corporal Anderson of the 73d regiment killed.

" I moved the matter to Monf. Fortuno, (French surgeon) concerning medicines, but he can give you no assistance at present; he says, when the hurry of this crisis is over he will be assisting. I had by me a small atom of Tartar Emetic, which I send per bearer. Give me leave once more, gentlemen, to make you a tender of my services, and to request that
" you

1783. " you will confide in me as in one who feels
" fenfibly for your fufferings."

The following letter fent to Serjeant Dempfter, in order that he may forward it. (From the Englifh officers confined in Seringapatam.)

" To the Governor or Commanding Officer
" of any Englifh fettlement.

" SIR,

" After a tedious and melancholy fe-
" clufion from our friends and the world,
" we have at length a profpect of tranfmit-
" ting fome account of ourfelves to thofe
" who muft but too fenfibly feel for our
" fituation, and be truly anxious for our
" lives and health.

" We do not know at which of our fet-
" tlements this letter will firft arrive, but
" requeft that the fum of one hundred pa-
" godas be inftantly paid on our account to
" the perfon who fhall deliver it; and that
" it be tranfmitted with all convenient fpeed
" to

" to the Governor of Fort St. George and 1783.
" the Commander in chief. We are all in
" good health, and, confidering the nature
" and length of our confinement, in tolera-
" ble fpirits; a gold fanam per day is our
" fole allowance for fubfiftence and every
" neceffary of life.

" We imagine, from the humanity Tip-
" poo Saib has generally fhewn to Euro-
" peans, that if our confinement be likely
" to continue much longer, an application
" to him for an increafe of allowance, and
" ftriking off our irons, might not be with-
" out effect. We fhould wifh, at the fame
" time, to be allowed medicines, and the at-
" tendance of the French furgeon, both of
" which have been for many months denied
" us; to which and our clofe confinement
" we muft chiefly attribute the death of
" thofe we have already loft.

" Colonel Baillie died on the 13th No-
" vember laft. He, Captain Rumley, and
" Lieutenant Frazer, were confined in a
" Choultry by themfelves, and were taken
" out

1783. "out of irons in March laft; the two lat-
"ter are well, but ftill kept feparate from
"us. Lieutenant Lind died here the 14th
"of April; Captain Lucas July 5th; Mr.
"Hope, cadet, the 7th; and Lieutenant
"Maconichy the 9th of the fame month.

"We earneftly requeft the Governor and
"Commander in chief to order copies of
"this letter to be fent to the feveral fubor-
"dinate fettlements and garrifons on the
"Coromandel coaft, as alfo by the firft
"fhips to Europe, with directions for its
"being publifhed in the London News-
"papers. We hope it is needlefs to enforce
"this requeft, by pointing out the many
"domeftic anxieties that muft arife from a
"total ignorance of our fate, and the me-
"lancholy effect that may be prevented by
"a knowledge of it.

"We beg leave to mention Lieutenant
"Gordon of Colonel Baillie's detachment,
"and Mr. Brunton taken at Pondicherry,
"who are confined with the foldiers by one
"of the many unaccountable acts of this
"govern-

" government, though repeatedly aſſured of 1783.
" their being officers. We have heard that
" Mr. M'Neale, mate of a country ſhip,
" and Mr. Wilſon, an officer of the Com-
" pany's cruizer Yarmouth, are alſo con-
" fined in the ſoldier's priſon.

" Sid Abram, commandant of the Tan-
" jore cavalry, is confined with us, and well
" merits the Honourable Company's re-
" membrance in the article for the return
" of priſoners. There is alſo a ſervant of
" one of the officers here, which makes the
" number of Europeans in this priſon a-
" mount to thirty-eight.

" P. S. From the death of Hyder, and
" the very different conduct of his ſon to
" ſuch Europeans as have fallen into his
" hands, we are induced to hope ſomething
" might be effected for the relief of ſuch
" officers and men as have been circumciſed
" and forced into the ſervice of Hyder Ally,
" though even a peace may be a more dif-
" tant event than his death gives us reaſon
" to hope. We therefore embrace this op-
" portunity

1783. "portunity of informing the government of
"Fort St. George, that they who have fuf-
"fered that misfortune, *at this place*, are as
"follows: *viz.* Lieutenants Speediman and
"Rutlidge; Enfign H. G. J. Jennings
"Clarke; Meff. Lefage, Auftin, Wilkin-
"fon, Drake, and Heideman, midfhipmen
"belonging to his Majefty's navy; eleven
"non-commiffioned and privates of the 73d
"regiment; forty-four feamen, King's and
"Company's; and about forty non-com-
"miffioned and privates of the Company's
"troops."

Jan. 12. The Keeladar of Nagram, Jad Bhie, has revolted and gone over to General Mathews.

13. Raifed by public fubfcription forty gold fanams, which we have fent to Captain Rumley and Lieutenant Frazer.

Tippoo Saib was in the Calicut country at the time his father died, and immediately on his hearing the news, he ordered a new Keeladar here, with one battalion of Sepoys, and

and proceeded himself (with Lally) to take 1783. charge of the army in the Carnatic. It was twenty-seven days from the time of his father's death until the time he took charge of the army, and every thing went on as smooth as before.

The whole of us turned out to satisfy the curiosity of a visitor; a black man of some consequence. Jan. 19.

Two Europeans and five Subadars, who were taken in the Tanjore country, have been obliged to carry mud, in order to force them to take service. 23.

Arrived Colonel Braithwaite and Ensign Holmes, not in irons. Arrived at the same time Captain Leech: he is confined in a different prison, with the daily allowance of six cash, and one sear of rice. 25.

Arrived prisoners two hundred and fifty Carnatic childern. 31.

The

1783.
Feb. 5.

The Verduvalla, at our requeſt, waited on the Keeladar, to acquaint him that we wiſhed to ſee him, or ſome head perſon, in order to lay before him our miſerable ſituation, being in want of medicines and nearly two years in irons.

6.

Viſited by the ſecond Myar, who ordered Lieutenant Sampſon's irons to be taken off, on account of his indiſpoſition.

Lieutenants Lindſey and Maſſey put in irons.

Sid Abram (our black Commandant), by the deſire of the whole, requeſted of the Myar to deliver the following particulars to the Keeladar.

1ſt. That we had been in heavy irons for near two years.

2d. That we had no medicines, nor were even allowed to purchaſe any for the relief of the ſick.

3d. That

3d. That we might be allowed one bottle of pia arrack for the ufe of the fick only, and to be kept always in charge of the centinel.

1783.

4th. That our allowance of a fanam per day was too fmall.

5th. That Mr. Skardon might be put on the fame allowance as the whole of us, he at prefent receiving only fix cafh, one fear of rice, half of doll, a little curry ftuff, and ghee per day.

To this we received no anfwer.

Muftered by the Myar, who particularly examined our irons.

Feb. 14.

Removed to Myfore, Captain Rumley, Lieutenants Frazer and Sampfon: poor Sampfon was exceedingly ill of an ague at the time he left us; we made up a fmall fum of forty gold fanams for him: ftrange are the conjectures concerning the fate of thefe three gentlemen.

26.

Four

1783.
Feb.
27.
Four European Muſſulmen detected, in attempting their eſcape.

Mar. 1. Received a letter from Colonel Braithwaite: he and Enſign Holmes are allowed one fanam per day each. Colonel Braithwaite having repreſented to us their miſerable ſituation, we in conſequence raiſed by public ſubſcription ſeventy gold fanams, and have deſired the Colonel to convey, if poſſible, part of the above ſum to Captain Leech, who we underſtand is ſtarving on ſix caſh per day: this unfortunate man was taken at Puddelotah, thirty miles from Trichinopoly, and is now confined along with two ſerjeants and three Subadars.

12. A letter ſent to the circumciſed Europeans a few days ago, and received the following anſwer.

" Dear Gentlemen and Countrymen,
" Your note we received, but ſorry we
" are to tell you that little ſatisfaction we
" can give you: no farther than to acquaint
" you that Nagram is ours. Captain Rumley
" and

" and two more officers were sent to Mysore. 1783.
" Gentlemen, we are sore oppreſt againſt
" our will to do as we do. You mention in
" your note about letters to the Carnatic,
" which we do not underſtand. Our army is
" about nine days march from this. Meſſrs.
" Speediman, Rutlidge, a ſerjeant major,
" and another ſerjeant, are all in irons at
" Gunjum Pett for attempting to make
" their eſcape."

Mahomed Ally, a General in Tippoo's Mar. ſervice, encamped ſix miles to the north- 14. ward of this, on his way to Nagram. His party conſiſts of five hundred French, two battalions of topaſſes, five battalions Sepoys, three thouſand horſe, with ſeveral guns.

Received a letter from Colonel Braith- 16. waite requeſting more fanams.

Two o'clock A. M. a total eclipſe of the 19. moon.

Sent

1782.   Sent Colonel Braithwaite thirty-four fanams, which we raised with the utmost difficulty.

Mar. 22.   Arrived the reliques of the late Hyder-Ally-Cawn, and interred in the Loll Bang garden, one mile east of the fort.

25.   Received a letter from Colonel Braithwaite, wherein he informs us that he has only received sixty fanams. A Verduvalla who was over the Colonel at this time, attended our prison on account of his indisposition; consequently we thought this a favourable opportunity to remit the money, and accordingly entrusted him; but found, to our sorrow, that he kept up forty fanams and two letters.

Apr. 1.   Colonel Braithwaite having pointed out a channel of corresponding with Tanjore, and wishing to have fifty fanams transmitted to him for that purpose, we have raised that sum by subscription, and sent it him, together with a list of our names, in order that they may be forwarded to our friends.

Received

Received the following letter from some 1783.
of the European Muffulmen.

"Dear Gentlemen,
"We intend to avail ourselves of the first
"opportunity to escape, as we would sooner
"die than remain in this rascal's service.
"If you should be released before we put
"this scheme in execution, pray be so good
"as consider our miserable situation."

Tippoo Saib passed this place for Nagram with a great part of his army. April 8.

The battalion of Carnatic slaves, who were drilled here by the European Muffulmen, have joined the army at Nagram. 21.

A salute fired for some favourable news received from Nagram.

Salutes fired, and sugar given to the inhabitants (guards go about with baskets full of sugar distributing it, like Roman dolls, among the people) and drums beating, in consequence of our having lost Nagram. May 1. 2.

The

1783.
May 6.
The person who engaged with Colonel Braithwaite to transact the correspondence with Tanjore, has declined to execute it.

16. The whole of us have subscribed half a fanam each per month to Captain Leech, which puts him on a level with us, as we understand he is in a most wretched situation.

June 19. Sent by the washerwoman to Captain Leech thirty-three gold fanams. Two months subscription.

20. A letter from Captain Leech acknowledging the receipt of thirty-two fanams.

Received the following letter from Brigadier-General Matthews, who arrived prisoner here the 27th of May, 1783.

" I am sorry for the misfortune of my
" friends. Rumley is dead. Fetherstone
" was killed. *I was* a Brigadier-General,
" and Commander in chief on the Malabar
" coast. Mangalore has a very good garri-
" son,

" fon, and I think will hold out till relieved 1783.
" from Madras. Our fleet is fuperior to
" the French in India. Our army victo-
" rious in the Carnatic; likewife in the
" Cuddapa country. Lang, a Brigadier-
" General, has taken Corrore, and has ten
" thoufand good men under him. Our af-
" fairs wear a tolerable afpect. The Mar-
" rattas have made a peace and alliance
" with us. I had three hundred Euro-
" peans and eight hundred Sepoys, effec-
" tive, at Nagram, called alfo Bedanore,
" and made a treaty with Tippoo, which
" he broke, plundered us, and made us
" clofe prifoners. I think that Tippoo
" wifhes for peace with us, and that fome-
" thing towards it may take place in No-
" vember. I am ufed ill, but not in irons.
" I have neither pen, ink, nor paper, and
" it is dangerous to correfpond. All the
" ftrong forts are in our poffeffion. I took
" the whole Malabar coaft. I brought
" from Bombay four hundred Europeans
" and one thoufand Sepoys, and was after-
" wards joined by the Calicut army. The
" number of places taken by me required

" all

1783. "all my troops to garrison, and I had not
"any support from any place. We knew
"not of your situation: if I had known it,
"I should not have been a prisoner. Ge-
"neral Stewart commands at Madras.—
"The troops that the French landed have
"been defeated. For myself and two Eu-
"ropean servants, and one black, I am al-
"lowed one fanam and a half per day, with
"one sear of meat, three of bad rice, and
"one of ghee. I am compelled ro receive
"what they give, and not allowed to buy
"any other from the Buzar. I cannot pro-
"cure any thing but through the Hircar-
"rah. Should any thing happen to my
"life, I wish you to remember, that the
"Company owe me, for money advanced
"by me during my command, thirty-three
"thousand rupees, besides all my pay, and
"allowance due from the time of my arri-
"val in India. The troops that were with
"me are some in the Nabob's service; the
"rest sent in irons to different parts of the
"country.

"RICHARD MATHEWS."

Saw

Saw the European Muſſulmen at drill this morning, on the parade; they gave us the compliment of the ſalam. 1783. May 30.

In honour of his Majeſty's birth-day, we had for dinner two quarters of ſtewed mutton, with a bread pudding; and drank his health in pure water. June 4.

Repeated applications to the Keeladar, in order to have ſeveral gentlemen's irons taken off, on account of their legs being ſwelled, and otherways indiſpoſed, but without ſucceſs. July 1.

Raiſed by ſubſcription twenty fanams, which we have given to the waſherman, for bringing General Mathews's letter, &c.

The whole of us have ſubſcribed one dub each for the Doctor's medicine box. This we do occaſionally. 23.

Received a letter from Colonel Braithwaite, of which what follows is an extract.

"Yeſterday

1783. " As we burn all your letters, we
" could be glad you would send us the
" names of those herbs good for sore legs.
" Captain Leech's are swelled, and very
" sore: he has no covering for them but old
" rags, from whence I conjecture that his
" w—— will let no cloth be bought for
" him; therefore it would be an act of cha-
" rity, if, amongst you, you would make up
" for him four suits of shirts and drawers,
" and deduct the money out of his next
" month's supply: you can send them from
" time to time by the waistcoat washer-
" man."

July 24.   Our servants, in going for water this evening, accosted a Subadar for news. This
man was formerly in our service. He desired the servants to give his particular salam
to us, and tell us to keep up our spirits,
for that we would very soon be released.

Sid Gofforr, who was a Commandant of
a battalion of Zebundy Sepoys, and taken
prisoner in the Tanjore country, is appointed

ed Commandant to a regiment of cavalry, 1783.
and allowed a palanquin. This is a particular mark of Tippoo's favour, as no one is permitted to make ufe of a palanquin, unlefs by exprefs orders from the Nabob.—Sid Gofforr, previoufly to his appointment, fent for his wife and children, as pledges of his fidelity.

This is a piece of policy very common among all the princes of India. If any perfon is diftinguifhed by fortune, by connections, or by any truft under government, care is taken that his family, or thofe who are moft dear to him, fhall be placed under the immediate obfervation of the prince, or the minifter in whom he confides. The head men, as they are called, of different villages, quarters of towns, &c. keeps regifters of all families of any note within their diftricts.

At five o'clock, P. M. receive intelligence of a project contrived in order to reinftate the King of Myfore. How dangerous foever this confpiracy might appear

1783. to be, yet every member at first appeared steady and undaunted. The parties who entered into this plot, were the Inchivalla, head post-master to Tippoo Saib, and keeper of the privy seals; the Prime Minister of the old King of Mysore; two Subadars; and nine other head-men. One of the Subadars had the command of one hundred men: the other had been a Subadar in Captain Keating's battalion, and taken prisoner on the fall of Amboor, a garrison in the Carnatic. The whole of the conspirators assembled several times, and after matters were arranged, they each swore solemnly to observe secrecy. Letters were then dispatched to our army at that time in the Combitore country, the Marrattas, and Corakees, requiring their assistance. Every thing promised success. They then agreed to disperse for the present, and to meet at the general rendezvouz about seven the same evening: but unfortunately for them, and likewise all the prisoners, the Subadar who had command of the hundred men instantly went to the Keeladar and informed him of the

the whole plot. Guards were ordered, and the whole party fecured and thrown into dungeons.

1783.

The firft object of the confpirators was, to have made fure of the Keeladar, the head Myar, and Afoff-Cawn; thefe three were to have been inftantly put to death: their next, to have releafed all the European and other prifoners, and then to have murdered the whole of Afoff-Cawn's battalion, the Sepoys of that corps having charge of all the prifoners, magazines, gates, &c.

A current report that we are all to be burned, as a retaliation for the lofs Tippoo has fuftained on the Malabar coaft.

Aug. 8.

Tippoo's fon, a lad about eight years of age, frequently takes an airing on horfeback in a ftreet adjoining to our prifon: which ftreet, fince the plot has been difcovered, is lined with centinels, and no one is allowed to pafs or repafs.

1783. On this occasion we peeped eagerly through some small apertures we had found means to make, or to improve a little, in the walls of our prison. The young Sultan was mounted on a beautiful managed Arabian horse, finely caparisoned. He was attended and preceded by a number of people, some of whom bore up his umbrella, others fanned his face, others proclaimed his rank and high descent. At one particular place by which he passed and repassed, two elephants were stationed to pay their compliments to the young prince among the rest of his adorers. The creatures were not only taught to kneel at his approach, and shew other marks of obedience, but to fan his face as he went along, with fans which they grasped and wielded with their trunk or proboscis.

Aug. 11. An addition to our guard of two troopers, and the Myar has visited our prison three times this morning, with orders to the guards to be particularly vigilant.

A

A most melancholy fight this morning: 1783. one of the conspirators stripped naked, and Aug. 14. dragged to death at an elephant's foot. In the afternoon two more of them, with their noses and ears cut off, riding on jack-asses, were hanged at the north gate of the fort.

The washerman acquaint us that Gene- 17. ral Mathews is put in irons.

Our Havaldar says peace is making. 19.

Received the following from Colonel 23. Braithwaite.

" Just as I had sent my dispatch to Ge-
" neral Mathews, his servants were brought
" to Leech's guard, where they now are,
" confined with him and the serjeant. They
" have half a fanam a-day between them,
" and the General, I suppose, is reduced to
" one: they were strictly examined by the
" Keeladar as to what the General's con-
" versation turned upon; particularly if the
" English did not want to make peace.—
" The washerman has informed me, that
" my

" my letters were safely delivered to the
" General. The General is put in irons."

We hear that eleven thousand horse have died in Tippoo's camp since his arrival on the Malabar coast, many elephants and camels, and a vast number of bullocks; and that his army in general is very sickly.

This day a list was made out of the following articles, fabricated by the English officers, prisoners with Hyder-Ally-Cawn, and Tippoo Sultan Bahadar, in Seringapatam.

 Hats of leather.
 Caps, of coarse dungeree.
 Stocks of ditto.
 Neckcloths of ditto.
 Banyan shirts, ditto.
 Jackets, ditto.
 Waistcoats, ditto.
 Trowsers, ditto.
 Socks, ditto.
 Buttons of thread.

          Tables

Tables of Bamboo, and covered with a mat.
Stools of ditto.
Cots of Bamboo, by the means of an old knife, converted into a saw; the cot lashed with coir rope, made from the cocoa nut.
Bird cages of Bamboo.
Trunks of ditto, 1100 pieces in one trunk.
Rat traps of ditto.
Squirrel traps of ditto.
Forks of ditto.
Back-gammon tables of ditto.
Dice, sawn with an old knife; the ivory acquired by stealth in the Buzar.
Chefs-boards, of paper and cloth.
Cards, two folds of paper, one of cloth, pasted together with thick conjee, and polished with the jaw-bone of a sheep.
Ink, of lamp-black, with a little gum-water. One chatty was placed over head of another, to collect the smoke of the taper or wick of a lamp, which was swept off every day.
Pens of fowl quills.

Paints,

1783. Paints, brought in by ſtealth,—indigo, red wool, and turmerick.

August 25. Sent Captain Leech a ſupply of thirty-four fanams per the waſherman.

Troops and guns arrived from Tippoo's camp, all corroborating the accounts of peace.

27. Our paymaſter ſays, that thirty heavy guns are arrived here, in conſequence of peace. This good man ſeems to take a pleaſure in giving us any information that may contribute to eaſe our ſituation.

Sep. 1. Saw forty of the European Muſſulmen at drill. Viſited by the Myar, and a Circar Bramin, who took all our names, with the rank, corps, and monthly pay of each.

8. The waſherman gives us the melancholy accounts of General Matthews's death. He died the 7th inſtant; and at the time he departed this life he was in irons. The waſherman further informed us, that he had

not

not changed his linen for twenty days, on account of his knowing that the Keeladar had mixed poison in the victuals he daily sent him. It appeared, indeed, from the treatment that the General at first met with, that Tippoo meant to use unfair means with him. Had he intended to use him agreeably to his rank, he ought to have allowed his staff to accompany him during his confinement: but so far from that, that he first broke a solemn treaty with the General and his officers. The General was then separated from the whole of his little captive army, brought here under a strong guard, thrown into a filthy dungeon; his baggage, cot, and every thing of the smallest consequence taken from him; his servants removed, and he himself thrown into heavy irons; and at last, to put a finishing stroke to the horrid scene, was dispatched by poison.

1783.

The General, when he learnt from a combination of suspicious circumstances, as well as hints let fall from those that were occasionally about his person, that it was the Sultan's intention to cut him off by poison,

1783. poison, refused to taste of the victuals that was sent to him at stated times from the Keeladar's. Some of the guards, and even the servants who carried the poisoned victuals, took compassion on the General, and gave him now and then a little of theirs. The Havaldar, who had the charge of the General, connived at these acts of humanity at first, and manifested symptoms of uneasiness and dissatisfaction with the part assigned to him in the scene going forward. But this officer, when it was found that General Mathews still protracted his miserable existence, was sent for by the Keeladar, who told him that the General's life, if much longer continued, must be paid for by the Havaldar's death. Upon this the Havaldar communicated his orders, with the threats that accompanied them, to his unfortunate prisoner, who had now no other alternative than that of perishing by famine or by poison. The anxious love of life maintained, for several days, a struggle with the importunate calls of furious hunger.—These, however, prevailed in the issue of the contest. He eat of poisoned food, and he

drank

drank too, whether to quench the rage of inflamed thirst, or to drown the torments of his soul in utter insensibility, of the poisoned cup. Within six hours after this fatal repast he was found dead. This is a faithful and true account of the death of Lieutenant-General Mathews, which has been set forth in various ways. The manner in which these particulars were brought to light was this:—The death of the General being reported to the Keeladar, it was mentioned, on that occasion, that a brass bason was found in his prison, with some writing on it: which must have been done with a fork he had with him. This was brought to the Keeladar, and read and interpreted by an European who had engaged in the Sultan's service.

The paymaster tells us, that peace is broke off, and that the Commandants of horse and infantry, contened in this vicinity, have received orders to recruit men with the utmost expedition.

The

1783.
Sep. 9.
The washerman says, that immediately on his delivering General Matthews's linen to the Circar, it was tore to pieces and thrown into the streets.

Arrived one regiment of regular black cavalry, consisting of five troops, fifty each. The horses given over to the Circar, and the troopers doing garrison duty.

18. The head Derroga of the slaves, who visits the Keeladar daily, is attended by nine of the European slave-boys who have been circumcised: each of them having a silver pearl in their right ear; this being a badge of slavery amongst the Mahometans.

19. The head Derroga appeared this evening on the terrace of Tippoo Saib's house, which has a flat roof with one turret on each corner, attended by five of the European slave-boys. On his perceiving us in the yard of our prison, he immediately called the unfortunate victims to the edge of the house, and particularly pointed us out to them.—
They

They were so very much affected that they burst into tears, and retired. The Derroga again brought them, and spoke to them in a very serious manner: we were not near enough to hear the conversation. It was the horror that the boys felt at the thought of being for ever shut out from the society of their countrymen, and the hope of returning to their country, that wrung their souls with tender anguish. The pain they felt was merely of this social kind, for, as far as we could judge from appearances, or from concurring reports, they were not subjected to any species of toil or drudgery, or to ill usage of any sort. They were, on the contrary, well clothed and fed, and supplied with every accommodation that was either necessary or convenient. They were sent to school to be instructed in the Persian language, in arithmetic, and algebra; and, in general, they were trained up in all the knowledge and accomplishments of the country, being intended for the household of the Sultan, and to be about his person. The officers, to whose care they were entrusted by the monarch, had orders to treat them

1783. them kindly, and to tell them that, being weaned from their attachment to the countries beyond the great ocean, and initiated in the religion of the holy Prophet, they would become the Sons of the Sultan, who would not fail to cherish, to bestow his confidence, and promote them in his service according to their merit.

Nor were these fair promises and expressions of kindness on the part of the Sultan, altogether insincere and affected. In India, where the human character possesses great sensibility of temper, ideas of adoption are quite familiar among the people: and the young ones that are adopted, dependent on the bounty, and obedient to the nod of the adopting parents, are embraced with all that affection which is usually shewn to real children. It was in this spirit that Nebuchadnezzar, King of Babylon, having reduced Judæa and carried the people captive into his own dominions, " Spoke unto Asphenaz the master of his " eunuchs, that he should bring *certain* " of the children of Israel and of the kings
" seed,

" feed, and of the princes children in whom 1783.
" was no blemish, but well favoured, and
" skilful in all wisdom, and cunning in
" knowledge, and understanding science,
" and such as had ability in them to stand
" in the King's palace, and whom they
" might teach the learning and the tongue
" of the Chaldeans. And the King ap-
" pointed them a daily provision of the
" King's meat, and of the wine which he
" drank: so nourishing them three years,
" that at the end thereof they might stand
" before the King.—Among these were of
" the children of Judah, Daniel, Hananiah,
" Mishael, and Azariah; unto whom the
" prince of the eunuchs gave names: for
" he gave unto Daniel the name of Belte-
" shazzar; and to Hananiah, of Shadrach;
" and to Mishael, of Meshech; and to
" Azariah, of Abed-nego *."

As a resemblance may thus be traced
between the situation of the sons of Judah
under Nebuchadnezzar, and those of Great

* Daniel I. 3—7.

1783. Britain under the Indian Monarch, so also, we discern an affinity between the feelings and emotions to which those situations unfortunately gave birth.—The tears and other signs of melancholy which were manifested to our view by the European slave-boys in the midst of ease and plenty, in the palace of a King! recalled to our thoughts how natural it was for the captive Jews of old, "To hang their harps on the willows, "to sit down by the rivers of Babylon, "and to weep when they remembered "Zion *."

Sep. 23. The paymaster assures us that peace is certainly made.

2. I saw some of the European slave-boys on Tippoo Saib's house: they paid us the compliment of the salam, made many melancholy signals with their hands, shed a flood of tears, and retired.

27. The annual Gentoo feast commenced this evening, which was continued, according to

* Psalm cxxxvii.

custom,

cuftom, for nine days. The King of Myfore made his appearance in a veranda, in front of his palace, about feven o'clock.

. This young prince, in whofe name the family of Hyder-Ally, who affume only the title of regent, carry on the adminiftration of government, is allowed, for himfelf and his family, an annual penfion of one lack of rupees. He is treated with all thofe marks of homage that are paid to crowned heads. In his name proclamation is made of war and of peace, and the trophies of victory are laid at his feet. Like kings, too, he has his guards: but thefe are appointed and commanded by the ufurper of his throne, whofe authority and fafety depend upon the prince's confinement. Yet fuch is the reverence that is paid by the people of Myfore to the blood of their antient Kings, and fo formidable are they rendered even in their prefent ftate of fubjection to the moft vigorous character as well as powerful Prince in the peninfula of Hindoftan, by their numbers, and the extent of their cities, efpecially of Seringapatam,

the

1783. the capital, which would faciliate their intercourse and co-operation, if any common principle or cause should spread the flames of discontent and insurrection, that it is thought expedient by the present government, not to cut off the hereditary prince of Mysore, according to the usual policy of despots, but to adorn him with the pageantry of a crown, to furnish him with all that is necessary to a life of sensual pleasure, to immerse him in voluptuousness, to unnerve his mind, and at stated times to present him, a royal puppet, to the view and acclamations of his people.

The spacious palace in which the young King of Mysore resides, stands in a large square, in the very centre of Seringapatam, in an angle of which our prison was also situated. Hence we had an opportunity of enjoying the sight of this annual festival, in which we were indulged during the whole time that it lasted. The prince, who is quite black, but exceedingly comely, appeared, as already mentioned, in a royal veranda or open gallery in front of his palace.
The

The curtains with which the gallery was hung being drawn up, difcovered the King feated on a throne, with numerous attendants on each hand; fome of whom fanned him, others fcattered perfumes on his long black hair, and on his cloaths, and others prefented his Hooker, replenifhed from time to time with betel, and other narcotics.— The veranda was decorated with the fineft hangings, and refplendent with precious ftones, among which a diamond of immenfe fize and value, fhone with diftinguifhed luftre. On a ftage extended in the open fquare, along the front of the palace, muficians, balladieres, and a fpecies of gladiators, entertained the King with his train in the gallery, and the multitude that filled the fquare, with mufic, dancing, tumbling, wreftling, mock-engagements, and other pantomimical diverfions. The ladies of his Majefty's haram, as well as the European prifoners, were, on this occafion, indulged with greater freedom than ufual, being allowed to enjoy the fpectacle, through lettice windows, as well as the other fubjects of Myfore. They were not black, but fair,

1783. fair, and exceedingly handsome. Their number seemed to be from forty to fifty. —The girls of Hyder's Seraglio, who were maintained by Tippoo, in their usual residence, after his death, amounted to the number of five hundred *.

The King having sat motionless in great state for several hours, rose up, when he was about to retire, and advancing to the edge of the gallery showed himself to the people, who honoured him with marks of the most profound and even superstitious veneration. The curtains then dropt, and his Majesty retired to the inner parts of the palace. It is only on occasion of this anniversary that the King of Mysore is visible to his nominal subjects.

Sep. 28. Saw forty of the European slaves at drill, under the charge of a black Commandant: very dirty and dejected.

A tom-tom went about this evening, forbidding any of the inhabitants to appear

* See Appendix, A.

in

in the streets after nine o'clock at night, on pain of losing their noses and ears.

1783.

Orders for a morning and evening gun to be fired in all Tippoo's garrisons.

The two men who were taken at Errode in 1768, Spencer and Wilton, passed our prison this morning, attended by a sentry. They were very indifferently dressed.

Oct. 1.

The Verduvalla of the guard informs us, that a Bramin of Tippoo's is gone to Madras concerning peace, and that two companies of Sepoys, of his, were in Mangalore, and two of ours in his camp. The Verduvalla thinks matters will be accommodated, as his master's affairs wear but a gloomy aspect, and that he has no confidence in his head men.

Several of our ships arrived at Mangalore with troops, and news that peace was broken off.

2.

Three

1-83.   Three of the men concerned in the late conspiracy, without their noses and ears, and riding on jack-asses, were hanged this morning.

Oct. 3.   The washerman gives us the melancholy news of Rumley, Frazer, and Sampson, being poisoned at Mysore.

4.   Shiek Rustan, Havaldar, who at one period commanded the guard of our prison, and one in whom we have great confidence, tells us that Rumley, Frazer, and Sampson, are all poisoned; and recommends to us to be particularly circumspect in our behaviour, or that we may meet with the same fate.

5.   Comrah, Sepoy, a Tanjore man, formerly on our guard, arrived this morning from Kavel Drook, and acquaints us that all the officers confined there have been poisoned, by express orders from Tippoo Saib. He believes there were eighteen or twenty of them.

Our

Our worthy friend the paymafter fays, 1783, that peace is on the eve of being concluded. Oct. 8.

Vifited by the Myar; he particularly en- 11. quired for our black Commandant's name, as alfo the officer's name who commanded the detachment in the Tanjore country, taken by Tippoo the 18th of February, 1782.

Received a letter by the wafherman from 12. Colonel Braithwaite, telling us that the wafherman had kept twelve of the fanams which we fent for the ufe of poor Captain Leech; as alfo of the death of Rumley, Frazer, and Sampfon: and that many of General Mathews's officers, confined at Kaval Drook, were dead, and the reft dying.

The wafherman, who is our conftant toppall, or poft, was a Havaldar in Captain Nixon's battalion, and taken prifoner the 10th of September, 1780, and took fervice in the ftyle of a wafherman (the men wafh and iron clothes): of courfe we had every reafon to fuppofe he would be affifting; but, on the contrary, he has taken every opportunity

1783. opportunity to pilfer us, although we have made him frequent presents, and promised him, on our enlargement, a Jemmidar's commiffion with a sum of money, provided he would not embezzle those fanams which we, with the utmost difficulty, raised for those in extreme distress.

Oct. 12. Colonel Braithwaite applied to the Keeladar for a cot to sleep on, but was refused.

The French have passed this place on their way to Pondicherry, in consequence, as we are informed, of a peace in Europe.

13. Lieutenant Butler, at the point of death, is allowed, after many applications, to have his irons taken off; and several other gentlemen are dangerously ill.

21. Sid Abram, our black Commandant, who had been bred up in our service, was this morning ordered to the kutcheree, and there told by the Keeladar, that it was Tippoo Saib's orders, that he should enter into his service; as also to give information where his

his wife and family were, in order that they might be sent for. The Keeladar advised him to take service without any hesitation, and observed, if he did not, that God only knew what would be the consequence. The Commandant was remanded back to our prison, and allowed to reflect on the business.

1783.

We have made up four shirts and four trowsers for Captain Leech, and have sent them by the washerman, together with twenty-four fanams. The fanams are put, or worked, into the buttons of the shirt, which we have contrived to deceive the washerman.

Oct. 22.

Seven European artificers, arrived here, are forced into Tippoo's service. They were selected from those men taken at Bednore or Nagram.

24.

Mirtozee, the commanding officer of the guard placed over our prison, who, by the humanity of his behaviour, had acquired our esteem, affection, and even confidence,

27.

corro-

1783. corroborates the melancholy tidings we had received of General Matthews's officers having, all of them, been carried off by poison at Kavel Drook, by the exprefs orders of the Sultan; which, he faid, was owing to the garrifon of Ananpore being all of them put to the fword by one of our European officers. He warned us of a fearch that was foon to be made in our prifon, for what we called contraband goods, fuch as razors, fciffars, knives, and other offenfive weapons; and papers, pens, and ink; the means of correfpondence and difcovery.

The commanding officer, to whom the inhuman tafk of poifoning our men at Kavel Drook was committed, having been often prefent with them, and of courfe been moved with compaffion, fuccefsfully exerted his influence to be removed from that ftation. The officer who had the charge of our foldiers prifon, at Seringapatam, was fent for to Myfore, and appointed in his ftead, with an exprefs charge to carry the orders and directions, that had been given for poifoning our men, into immediate execution. This being

being done, the officer returned to his charge 1783. of our foldiers prifon at Seringapatam, which he occafionally vifited as ufual. Certain of our men, who had heard fome furmifes of the horrid purpofe for which he had been abfent, and who were moved with the livelieft inquietude and apprehenfions, ventured to put the queftion to him, Why they had fo long been deprived of the honour of his vifits? He made not the leaft fcruple to tell them the fhocking bufinefs in which he had been employed, apologizing, at the fame time, for his conduct, by obferving, that if he had not obeyed orders, he would himfelf have been put to death.

Colonel Braithwaite has received a cot and fome Margoza bark, from the Keeladar; and was at the fame time defired to apply for any thing he wanted. The Colonel requefted he might be removed to us, or fee the French Doctor, as alfo to fit on the outfide of the prifon door, during the time his fervants were dreffing his victuals. The Keeladar to thefe demands gave an evafive anfwer.

Oct. 29.

Received

1783.
Oct.
30.

Received the following from Colonel Braithwaite.

"Colonel Braithwaite presents his compliments to the Gentlemen, has received four shirts, four drawers, for Captain Leech, but no *pills*, meaning fanams*, are to be found. He begs to know how they were sent. The Colonel takes the liberty to send them a few lines, by way of epitaph, on his late friend Sampson, which he hopes his friends will wear in their hearts, as his destiny denies him a tomb-stone. It is the only tribute the Colonel can now pay to the memory of an officer, whom he brought up and loved with parental affection. Should he survive his captivity, he will demand his bones, and those of the other gentlemen, who have died here, and carry them to Madras for interment."

* The fanams were put in the buttons, the washerman at this time had not an opportunity of delivering them.

SAMPSON

SAMPSON here rests his head on hostile earth ; 1783.
A youth to fortune, not to fame, unknown :
The former frowned even at his birth,
The latter surely mark'd him for her own.
How great his bravery, let beholders tell :
Much did he do, and to the last did try.
Active, amidst out-numb'ring foes he fell—
Disabled—too luckless! then to die
A wounded captive in barbarians chains!
Uncommon rigour mark'd his cruel fate;
A tyrant's caution caus'd his latest pains :
At length he died, a long, long year too late.
Lay light upon him earth ; and may his God
With mercy meet him, and for ay reward,
A youth, who in the walk of honour trod ;
Yet suffer'd here, alas! a lot too hard.

Serjeant Higgins (who voluntarily took service) with two other European Mussulmen, have made off to Mangalore from Nagram ; but one of the three was unfortunately detected. Nov. 1.

The European Mussulman taken in endeavouring to make his escape, was shot in Tippoo's camp, and six more of the European Mussulmen, who were also in his camp, are ordered to Shittle Drook. 2.

1783.
Nov.
3.

The Europeans given up by the French were at drill this morning, and attended by four Havaldars.

All the Europeans who have been made Muffulmen are confined in a large fquare, and no one is permitted to go out without a fentry.

Our allowance of one fanam per day (or eleven dubs) is reduced to nine dubs and two cafh, a lofs of fix cafh each per day; which affects us in the moft ferious manner. We fhall be puzzled how to exift. Mr. Skardon has received an addition of three cafh per day.

4.

The European Muffulmen, and black flaves, are given in charge of the black officers of cavalry, whom they are to inftruct in the infantry duty; a moft melancholy fight to us. All this is owing to Monfieur Suffrein.

The Inchivalla, who was the ring-leader 1783 in the confpiracy, ftill remains in heavy irons, and on low diet.

About ten this morning, fifty of the European Muffulmen, with firelocks, and a body of native troops, efcorted the Keeladar to a mofque, one mile weft of the fort. They were commanded by a black officer, who frequently, in our hearing, called out to them, as they were paffing our prifon, *Chillow Feringee Banjoot* *, with other expreffions of infolence and contempt. — Nov. 8.

The paymafter informs us, that Mangalore is given up in confequence of peace; that Tippoo is to be here in eight days; and that an officer of rank is on his way from Madras, in order to receive the prifoners. The paymafter has affured us in the ftrongeft manner, that the above information is undoubted, and requefts that we would, on our enlargement, make him a fmall falam, which he intends to appropriate to his — 9.

* Go on, ye white flaves.

daughter's

1783. daughter's marriage.* This good man is deserving of every thing we can do for him,

as

* In Hindostan, the expence of clothes is almost nothing; and that of food, firing, and lodging, to the native, very trifling. The Hindoos are not addicted to any expensive vices, their passions and desires being gentle and moderate. Yet they are frugal and industrious, and as eager to amass riches as any of the natives of Europe. A Jew, a Dutchman, or a Scotch pedlar, is not more attentive to profit and loss. What is the reason of this? They are lovers of splendour and magnificence in every thing, but particularly in what relates to their women. It is in their harams, but especially on occasion of their marriages, that they pour forth the collected treasures of many industrious years. It may also be proper to observe, here, that the good man, who had expressed a concern for the due celebration of his daughter's marriage, had in his eye, and even knew for certain, the family and the youth to whom she was to be married.

Marriages are contracted by boys and girls, and consummated as soon as they arrive at puberty; that is, when the men are from twelve to thirteen years of age, and the women nine or ten. The marriage ceremony is performed three times; once when the couple are mere infants; a second time, when the gentleman may be about eight or nine years old, and the lady five or six; and the third and last time, at the age I have already specified. Between the first and second marriage ceremonies, the young couple are allowed to see one another: they run about and play together as other children do; and knowing they are destined for each other, commonly

as he has on every occasion shewn humanity and attention towards us.

The paymaster's news corroborated from all quarters.

Six o'clock, P. M. departed this life Lieutenant Butler. This unfortunate man was sick for near six months, and although the two Myars saw his wretched situation,

monly conceive, even at that early period, a mutual affection. But after the second time of marriage, they are separated from each other; the bride, especially if she be a person of condition, being shut up in the women's apartment until the happy day of the third and last ceremony, when the priest sprinkles on the bride and bridegroom a bundance of rice, as an emblem of fruitfulness.

These early contracts are undoubtly well calculated to inspire the parties with a mutual and lasting affection. The earliest part of life is in every country the happiest; and every object is pleasing that recals to the imagination that blessed period. The ductile minds of the infant lovers are easily twined into one; and the happiest time of their life is associated with the sweet remembrance of their early connection. It is not so with your brides and bridegrooms of thirty, forty, and fifty: they have had previous attachments; the best part of life is past before their union, perhaps before they ever saw each other.

1783. and repeated applications were made to the Keeladar for medicines, and a little Pia arrack, yet the cruel barbarian gave no kind of affiftance, but allowed him to linger out a life of mifery and wretchednefs.

The wafherman having made a demand of eight dubs for bleaching the fhirts and drawers fent to Captain Leech, we have, in confequence of his application, raifed that fum by a fubfcription of one cafh each.

Two divifions of the European Muffulmen were at drill this morning, each divifion commanded by a black officer.

Nov. 9. The funeral fervice was this morning read over the late Lieutenant Butler, who was carried out as decently as the prifon would admit of.

The Keeladar fent for the effects of the late Lieutenant Butler, confifting of a few old rags. The Verduvalla took as much care in examining them, as if they had been of the utmoft confequence.

Preparations

Preparations making, such as white-washing the houses, cleaning the streets, &c. in order to receive Tippoo Sultan Bahadar. 1783. Nov. 10.

An officer of rank expected here to-morrow, to receive the prisoners: a Choultry and Pandall* fitted up for his reception, one mile north of the fort, at a village called Soomer Pettah. 11.

The European Muſſulmen were at drill this morning, and mixed in the ranks with the black ſlaves. They and the black ſlaves have had their right ears bored, in order to wear the Mahomedan badge of ſlavery, which is a ſilver pearl. 12.

Colonel Braithwaite paſſed our priſon on his return from the Keeladar. He was well dreſſed, and under charge of one Havaldar and twelve Sepoys, with fixed bayonets.— Several of us were ſo rejoiced at ſeeing him, 15.

---

* A kind of portico for making the Choultry cooler, formed by wooden poles, and the leaves and branches of trees.

1783. that they forgot their situation, and called out to him, by name, through holes they had bored through the wall of the prison. The Colonel was astonished, and some of the prisoners disapproved of this conduct of their companions. But their emotions were so lively, that they could not be restrained.

Various and uncertain accounts of peace: one moment we are informed that peace is finally concluded; the next, there is fighting; and in this miserable situation are we daily tortured with alternate hopes and fears, which produce a state of anxious and painful suspense.

The Corakees have defeated a party of Tippoo Saib's troops at Perripatam, nineteen miles west of this, and a reinforcement of Chaylahs and Colleries are ordered from hence to reinforce them.

Nov. 16. The reduction of our allowance of the six cash has so materially affected our mode of living, that we are obliged now to breastfast on two cash of conjee and two cash cafh of milk. Two dinners in the week 1783. of doll pepper-water, each dinner nine cafh; one ditto of cutcheree, twelve cafh, two mutton curreys, and two foup dinners.

Forty Europeans and two battalions of black flaves with firelocks (no bayonets) marched out of the fort at two o'clock in the afternoon, in order to be reviewed by the Keeladar; the European flaves were divided in the ranks with the Chaylahs, very dirty, and but indifferently dreffed. Some had hankerchiefs on their heads, others turbans, and from their mid-thigh downwards they were entirely naked. Surely no fituation on earth is equal to theirs: however we flatter ourfelves that whenever we meet with that happy hour of liberty, and their cafe is made known, every ftep will be taken in order to recover them from flavery and Mahomedanifm. The Europeans and black flaves have all a filver pearl in their right ear. Nov. 17.

The Keeladar with the flaves returned at eleven this night.

Colonel

1783.
Nov.
18.

Colonel Braithwaite informs us by letter, that he has only received twenty fanams from the wafherman on account of Captain Leech. The wafherman has taken the remainder: this villain's cunning outreaches all our fchemes. The Colonel and Enfign Holmes's allowance reduced to nine dubs and two cafh each per day, and Captain Leech and the ferjeant are raifed to ten cafh each. The Colonel daily fends Captain Leech a fix cafh breakfaft.

Five Europeans, hand-cuffed, arrived prifoners from the Durma country.

19. Received the following from Colonel Braithwaite.

" When I got near the Keeladar's houfe,
" a man came out in a great hurry and
" feeming agitation, to fay it was a miftake,
" and ordered me back. In repaffing your
" prifon-houfe, I heard you fay, by G—d
" there's Colonel Braithwaite: upon which
" I anfwered in fome fuch exclamation. I
" had a very pleafant walk, and faw much
" of

" of the city, which is the fineſt I have 1783.
" ſeen in India. Soon after I got back to
" my dungeon, two or three perſons came
" from the cutchery, to tell me, whatever
" clothes or money I wanted, to aſk and I
" ſhould have. I ſaid, whatever the Na-
" bob allowed me I would receive; if ten
" pagodas a-day I would ſpend them; if
" ten caſh I would live upon it. I would
" aſk for no money; clothes I ſhould be
" glad of. Three pieces of tolerable cloth
" for ſhirting has been ſent me; they ſay a
" taylor is to come to-day. This change
" in regard to me looks well. Two preſſed
" taylors are come; they pretend they can-
" not do my work; but I believe the chau-
" buck will teach them. I have ſeriouſly
" declared I will not pay them."

Our good friend Mirto Jee ſays, that Nov.
peace is certainly broken off. 20.

The Commandant aſked the Verduvalla
for news. He gave him for anſwer, that the
news was very cold.

Captain

1783. Captain Judfon has received thirteen pagodas by the hands of an old woman, come to Seringapatam in fearch of her fon, a Sepoy in our fervice, which was fent with a letter by Mrs. Judfon, his wife, from Trichinopoly. The old woman, ever fince the fatal battle near Conjeveram, had wandered in a continued ftate of pilgrimage, not being able to reft long in one place, under the anxious and tender concern that inwardly preyed on her maternal breaft. After vifiting every place that report had fuggefted as the probable fcene of her fon's confinement, if in life, fhe at laft made her way to Seringapatam, where fhe found him; and we all of us participated in her joy. The woman faithfully delivered the money which Mrs. Judfon had committed to her care, to our fervants, whom fhe found at the well, where they attended daily to fetch water, and which had become a kind of poft-office. Mrs. Judfon, we were fometimes inclined to think, muft have received by fome means or other a defcription of the well. But if this had been fo, how could we account for the commanding officer at Trichinopoly's

not

not taking the fame opportunity of corre- 1783.
fpendence that was embraced by Mrs. Judfon? The attention of government, indeed,
could not well be expected to equal the
cares of maternal and conjugal affection.

This is the only letter or money received
in Hyder's country from our friends.

Captain Judfon receives through the old Nov.
woman a letter from Mrs. Judfon, dated the 21.
14th of laft month, in anfwer to one he
wrote in February laft, acquainting him
that he might expect to be fupplied from
time to time with money, and that there
was a talk of peace.

The guard that was ftationed over the 27.
European officers, prifoners at Kaval Drook,
returned here three days ago, and gave us
the melancholy account of all General
Matthews's officers being poifoned.

A Circar Verduvalla with armourers,
this morning, particularly examined our
irons. The Verduvalla corroborated the
account we had received of the dreadful
catastrophe

1783. cataſtrophe of the officers at Kaval Drook; as alſo of Rumley, Frazer, and Sampſon, at Myſore; and ſaid, that he made no doubt but that the Nabob would poiſon all the Engliſh priſoners

Several thouſands of troops, and moſt of them Carnatic people, are drilling here, for the cavalry, artillery, and infantry. Tippoo copies our mode of diſcipline in every reſpect.

Dec. 1. The nine ſlave-boys, who attend the Derroga, are intended for the Nabob's family.

4. Arrived priſoners, twenty Europeans, and two European women, chained two and two.

5. Arrived priſoners, twelve Europeans, chained two and two, they were ſhipwrecked on the Malabar coaſt.

10. The Subadar who impeached the conſpirators, is made a Commandant of Colleries,

ries, and has received many other favours from the Nabob: we have part of his battalion over us, and he frequently vifits the prifon, and feems very anxious to enter into a converfation; however, as he has been particularly pointed out to us by fome of our friends, we act with caution.

1783.

Colonel Braithwaite acquaints us, that he has repeatedly applied to the Keeladar for a greater allowance, and for taylors, but without fuccefs.

A European officer, who was taken prifoner on this coaft about two months after the fall of Nagram, and fent here, is circumcifed and appointed Commandant to a battalion of Chaylahs: we have not been able as yet to learn any thing farther concerning this unfortunate man,

Dec. 12.

This evening, the whole of the European Muffulmen were marched to Myfore. Seven miles fouth.

19.

Received

1783.
Dec.
21.
Received from the Keeladar two Banyans two short drawers, and a sheet; they were made of the coarsest dungeree, and the same quality as delivered out to the black slaves; so very unfit for our purpose, that we begged of the Verduvalla to return them, and endeavour to procure us a piece of cloth each in their stead: the cloth to be about four or five fanams per piece. On the Verduvalla's reporting this to the Keeladar, he replied, Very well, that we might wait a few days. Strange are the conjectures which are formed concerning this present, as it is the only instance of generosity we have met with from that quarter, during our imprisonment: it has made a number of gentlemen very melancholy—apprehensive of force to take service. Not like peace.

22. Many of our guards assure us that we are all to be circumcised, and taken into the Nabob's service; and that the dungeree we received yesterday was given in consequence of that resolution.

Captain Judson has sent two pagodas to Colonel Braithwaite.

Sent

Sent by the washerman Captain Leech's supply, thirty-one fanams. A current report of peace, and that our ambassadors from Madras are only a few days march from this.

1783.

Received a letter from Colonel Braithwaite, acquainting us that he has only received twenty-four fanams for Captain Leech.

Reports of our ambassadors being at Malvaree, twelve cofs N. E. of this place; that they have applied to the Keeladar to send us money and clothes; but that the Keeladar would not comply with their request, as he observed that he had no *hookum*, or order, from the Nabob.

Dec. 29.

Three Europeans, who were taken at, or near, Calicut about two months ago, and sent here, are forced into the barbarian's service as stone-cutters.

The two men, Spencer and Wilton, who were taken at Errode, passed our prison.

30.

1783.
Dec.
31.

The Verduvalla, by an order from the Keeladar, told Sid Abram that he muft confent to enter into the Nabob's fervice, and give an account where his wife and family were, that they might be fent for. The Commandant replied, that he had, from his boyifh days, been brought up amongft the Englifh, had met with every attention and encouragement that a foldier merited, and that he would on no account give information where his wife and family were, nor would he confent to enter into the Nabob's fervice.

A meffage, or falam, from Meer Nazer Ally, formerly an officer in our fervice, but who had fallen prifoner and taken fervice, to Sid Abram, that peace was certainly concluded, and applauding him for his fteady conduct in refufing to take fervice. Meer Nazer Ally was a Subadar in Captain MacAlifter's regiment of cavalry, and taken prifoner with Lieutenant Crewitzer; he now commands a regiment of cavalry, and is doing duty here.

The

Our guards doubled and the centinels particularly vigilant.- A report prevails that we are all to be put to death. 1784. Jan. 13.

The two troopers who came on our guard at the time of the confpiracy, were this morning relieved. 14.

The whole of us turned out in order to be muftered by a Subadar fent by the Keeladar.

Abdull Ruffel, Commandant to Captain Alcock's battalion, and taken prifoner with Colonel Braithwaite, was fent to Arneé and thrown into heavy irons, on three cafh per day, and one fear of raggee, becaufe he would not enter into the barbarian's fervice: many others, for the fame reafon, were treated in the fame manner, until they confented to take fervice, and fend for their families. 22.

A European boy about twelve years of age informed our fervants at the well this evening, that he belonged to his Majefty's thirty-fecond or forty-fecond regiment, that he 24.

1784. he was taken prisoner at Nagram, and since circumcised. His name is Lindsey.

Jan. 27.   The Inchivalla was this morning publickly flogged, near our prison, and his back rubbed with chilleys, or cayenne pepper.

Arrived from Mangalore, thirty elephants with their howders.

29.   The nine circumcised European boys still remain under the charge of the Derroga; two of them were this morning on the terrace of Tippoo Saib's house: they made signals that the Nabob would be here in fifteen days, and that we should then be released. We were greatly affected by their repeated melancholy signs of their situation: on their retiring they shed a flood of tears, and took off their turbans.

An increase of our allowance of one cash per day, owing to the exchange of the fanam.

Arrived

Arrived from Mangalore eight elephants, 1784. with their howdars; a species of frame fix- Feb. 1. ed to the elephant for fitting on—a little tent with curtains.

The Europeans who were shipwrecked, 2. and arrived here in December, are chained two and two, with the daily allowance of one fear of rice and two pice each.

At four this evening five of the European Feb. 4. boys under the charge of the Derroga were on the terrace of Tippoo's house, and made many tokens of their wretched situation.

The whole of us turned out, in order to be mustered by the Myar and a Bramin, as also our servants.

Visited by the Myar and a Bramin, who took our names, together with those of our servants. Many gentlemen alarmed on this occasion.

Spencer and Wilton passed our prison this morning

1784. morning. The European Muſſulmen ſtill remain at Myſore.

We have diſpatched a letter by the waſherman to the unfortunate men who arrived here a few days ago, requeſting to know in what manner they fell into the enemy's hands, and offering our aſſiſtance in money, to the amount of fifty fanams.

Received the following from one of them, Mr. Lilly.

" I have been in priſon going on ſeven
" months. We were brought up here du-
" ring the ceſſation of arms in irons, upon
" one pice and one ſear of rice per day;
" upon our arrival here they gave us two
" pice per day, and put all in irons, only
" two men who were ill, and they excuſed
" me. There is no officer here, only one
" ſurgeon, a foreigner, whoſe name is King,
" and one who follows the civil line; and
" I was taken as I came to buy a ſhip at
" Mangalore. There are fourteen Euro-
" pean ſoldiers, beſides about thirty Sepoys,
" that

" that were caſt away in a gale of wind, 1784.
" who were taken as priſoners.

" LILLY."

Mr. Lilly's letter not proving ſatisfactory, we have in conſequence forwarded another.

Fourteen Subadars, or Captains, and a number of Sepoys, have been carrying mud for many months paſt, in order to force them to take ſervice. Feb. 13.

A European boy informed our ſervants at the well this evening, that he, with nine more, were taken priſoners at Nagram; that they were drummers and fifers of his Majeſty's 101ſt and 102d regiments; that they had been circumciſed; and were at preſent under the charge of the head Derroga, Haſſin Ally Cawn. The boy earneſtly requeſted of the ſervants, that they would inform us that they were uſed barbarouſly; and hoped that, upon our enlargement, we would take an active part in repre- 14.

1784. representing to the government of Madras their wretched situation.

Feb. 15. Our servants again saw the European boy at the well, and assured him, by our desire, that every exertion in our power should be made on our enlargement; and requested an account of himself and comrades in writing. He replied, none of them could write.

18. We are informed that the name of Tippoo's eldest son is Abdull Ally Bahadar.

19. Sixty-seven circumcised Europeans are at Mysore. Messrs. Speediman, Rutlidge, Serjeant-major Groves, with several others, still remain at Gunjum Pettah.

Received the following from Mr. Lilly.

" Gentlemen,

" The cessation of arms took place with
" Tippoo Saib the 2d of August for four
" months. We were sent up here before
                                            " the

" the expiration of it. I cannot tell how 1784.
" they managed the other part of the nego-
" tiation. The negotiators for peace were
" not arrived in camp when we came away;
" but it is certain they arrived here the 25th
" December: they expected them in camp
" when we came away. Tippoo carried
" his guns to the brink of the ditch; he
" attempted ftorming twice, and was re-
" pulfed with great lofs; they were fo
" clofe in fome places, that our people
" threw fourteen-inch fhells over the
" breaft-work out of their hands upon the
" French. The fea don't wafh the walls
" of Mangalore. Two thoufand Europeans
" have arrived from Europe laft year. Ge-
" neral Stewart commands at Madras. The
" firft battalion of Sepoys was taken at Na-
" gram, but Captain Bowles went up to
" Bombay before they were taken. I am
" exceedingly obliged to you for your kind
" offer. I am not in want of cafh at pre-
" fent; if I fhould, I'll make bold to trou-
" ble you; but we are all in expectation
" of being releafed in a few days, as we
" have been muftered twice, and our names
" taken

1784. "taken to fend to Tippoo, in order for our
"enlargement.

"Mr. King thanks you for your kind
"offer; he is not in much want of cafh as
"yet; he has not a grain of Tartar Eme
"tic, but can fend you fome Ipecacuana,
"with fome Bark, if you fhould want it."

14th February.

A fubfcription of twenty-eight fanams, in order to requite the wafherman for the letters carried to and from Mr. Lilly.

Feb. 20. Sent Captain Leech a fupply of eighteen fanams.

The fubfcriptions of late have come fo heavy on us, that we are obliged to make four dinners in the week of rice and ghee, each dinner feven cafh.

21. Two Sepoys who are at prefent attached to our guard, have given us the melancholy accounts of our brother-fufferers at Kaval Drook. They fay that the Keeladar of Kaval

val Drook received orders from the Bahadar 1784. to difpatch the whole of them with poifon; that the Keeladar made no fecret, but explained his orders, and obferved, that unlefs they were inftantly put in execution, his own life would pay for his difobedience. The firft he called pofitively refufed to tafte the poifon. The Keeladar inftantly ordered feveral Coffres to feize and tie him up to a tamarind tree. After being moft feverely flogged, he at laft confented to drink the finifhing draught. Many others were flogged and inhumanly treated, on account of their oppofition. The Sepoys obferved, that the fcenes of diftrefs, after the poifon began to operate, were beyond defcription; fome being perfectly infenfible, others thrown into violent convulfions, and others employing the few moments they had to live in committing themfelves to God, and in embracing and taking a laft farewell of their companions and friends. Immediately after the whole were difpatched, the armourers knocked off their irons, and their bodies were then thrown into a wood as a prey for tygers.

Wrote

1784.
Feb.
27.
Wrote to Mr. Lilly, requesting he would be very circumspect in writing, as a detection might prove fatal to us all.

29. Report of Tippoo's having got possession of Mangalore by stratagem: this has damped our prospects, and diffused gloomy ideas in prison.

Received some medicine from Mr. Lilly, brought by the washerman, for which we gave him two fanams.

March 1.
The whole of us ordered to fall in, in order to be mustered by a Myar and a Bramin: they say that peace is broken off, and that we are to be sent to Kaval Drook.

2. In consequence of yesterday's information relative to our being sent to Kaval Drook, the whole of us have seriously and unanimously determined to avail ourselves of the first opportunity to make our escape, by murdering the whole of our guards, and selling every drop of blood as dear as possible; being

being thoroughly convinced, that if we submit tamely, we shall, on our arrival at Kaval Drook, be dispatched in the same manner as General Mathews's officers.

1784.

One of the circumcised European boys informed our servants at the well this morning, that peace is broken off.

Received the following letter from the soldiers prison, written by a black man; the same who had been interpreter to the Keeladar of the above-mentioned particulars respecting the death of General Matthews.

March 7.

" Since my arrival here, I have instructed
" myself to learn English from a spelling-
" book which I purchased from a European,
" which is now entirely broke to pieces; I
" therefore humbly beg the favour, if you
" have any book of any sort to spare, to send
" me by the bearer, that will be a means of
" my not losing what little I have learned. I
" must inform you, that my teacher, Serje-
" ant Hillingsworth, departed this life about
" twelve months ago. The Europeans ta-
" ken with Colonel Baillie join with me in
" their

1784. "their duty to you, and all their officers,
" Serjeant Brazier sends his duty to Cap-
" tains Mentieth and Wragg, and to inform
" them that there is himself and eleven pri-
" vates remaining here: Serjeant Macor-
" mick deceased the 29th of December,
" 1782. All the news we have is, that it
" is a peace, and that some of our gentle-
" men is with the Nabob, and expected
" here daily. At about eight or nine
" months ago, a poor distressed European
" woman, with a fine boy, and big with
" child, taken in Nagram, belonging to a
" serjeant of grenadiers of the hundredth
" regiment; since which she has been de-
" livered of a girl: her allowance is one
" pice and one sear and a half of rice per
" day. About six months ago twenty-seven
" Europeans of the different regiments were
" taken on the Malabar coast, and sent a-
" mongst us, which makes in all sixty-two
" Europeans: our allowance is two pice
" and one sear of rice per day.
                " VANKATACHELLIEM."

The

The guards acquaint us, that several black 1784. prisoners have been taken out in the dead of the night, and murdered, and that they seriously felt for our situation.

In consequence of the miserable situation of the European woman and her two infants, we have raised with the utmost difficulty twenty gold fanams; and at the same time have assured her, that we will on every occasion be assisting.

At nine o'clock, P. M. Sid Abram, our March black Commandant, was by an order from 7. the Keeladar removed from our prison.— This truly good man was exceedingly affected at his being separated from us, and frequently requested, that, whenever we should be enlarged, we would remember him to his wife and mother; as he never would consent to enter into the barbarian's service, which would of course prevent him from ever seeing his family.

Sid Abram, with twelve other black of- 9. ficers, taken prisoners since the commence-

ment

1784. ment of the war, are all in irons, with the daily allowance of three cafh and one fear of raggee.

One of our gentlemen alarmed us all exceedingly by a fit of infanity, during which he raved on the fubjects that moft concerned us all, and that were uppermoft in our minds. He had been afflicted with feveral fits before this time; but we always endeavoured to conceal his fituation from the Havaldar of the guard, being apprehenfive that he would have him removed from our prifon to fome place of confinement, which folitude, and perhaps other circumftances, might render ftill more difmal. This day, however, he was extremely ill: and made repeated application to the Havaldar to have an interview with the Keeladar, to whom, he faid, he had fomething to communicate of the laft importance. This alarmed us exceedingly: for when we reflected on the conftant fears of the barbarians, left we fhould make our efcape either by force or fraud, or find means of communicating fome ufeful intelligence to our countrymen,

countrymen, and at the same time considered 1784. that so many of our officers, soldiers, and Sepoys, had been slaughtered in cold blood by the sword, or forced to die by poison; there was not a doubt that the discovery of our utensils, our correspondence with the other prisons, and some parts of our conversation, would be followed by certain and speedy death. We judged it expedient, in the present extremity, however much against our inclinations, to acquaint the Havaldar that he was really insane. This the Havaldar would not believe; but affirmed that we all of us told lies, as he concluded, he said, from the circumstance that the gentleman discoursed to him with perfect reason and propriety. The insane person, unfortunately for us, spoke the Mahomedan language with great fluency: if he had not, we could have told our own story.

We endeavoured to reason with the Havaldar, and mentioned many particulars in our own vindication, in vain. We then requested that our servants might be called, and examined whether they had not frequently

1784. quently perceived him in a state of insanity, before this time. They were accordingly called, and they confirmed every thing that we had said. The Havaldar then said, that he believed there was some truth in what we had asserted, but that he must make a report of what had happened. We entreated of him to make as favourable an one as possible, as we would be exceedingly happy, if our fellow-officer, though unhappily disordered in his understanding, should be removed from us.

The Havaldar requested, and insisted with him to declare what he had to say. But this he refused to do, again and again, saying that he would not communicate the important business to any other person than the Keeladar, and that he would be revenged on the whole of us, as we were a set of villains and rascals, and that we had made many attempts to poison him. In fact, he had frequently entertained ideas of this kind, and would often attend and overlook the servants while they were employed in dressing the victuals. It was fortunate for us, us, and the circumstance, beyond all doubt, which, under Providence, saved our lives, that his madnefs turned upon poifon, and not upon our having papers, journals, knives, fciffars, and other things concealed, and, above all, on our fecret correfpondence with the other prifons.

Several gentlemen endeavoured to reafon with this unhappy man, to no purpofe.— In the courfe of the evening the Havaldar waited on the Keeladar to acquaint him that an Englifh officer, in one of the prifons, wifhed anxioufly to fee him, having fomething to communicate to him of the greateft confequence. The Havalder was defired to come again to the Keeladar next morning.

From the time that the infane perfon applied to the Havaldar, we were bufily employed in burning papers, digging holes in the ground in which we might hide things, and in putting things under the tyles of the prifon, until we fhould have an opportunity of burning them afterwards. During the courfe

1784. courſe of the evening we burned upwards of one hundred ſheets of paper, which we had got in by ſtealth, in order to amuſe ourſelves by learning different languages *. The people who brought in theſe things for us, were equally alarmed with us, and dreaded the fatal conſequences of a diſcovery.

The inſane perſon, with a pair of irons of about eight pounds in weight, began to walk about in the priſon at five o'clock in the evening, and continued to walk, at a great pace, without ceaſing, till two o'clock in the morning, raving all the while, and vowing vengeance againſt all his fellow-priſoners. The ſtate of our minds, on that horrible night, is not to be deſcribed. It was propoſed at one time to put him inſtantly to death, and, by that ſacrifice, to

* In Hindoſtan the children of the common people are taught reading and arithmetic in the open air: and they learn to diſtinguiſh the letters and figures they uſe by forming them with their own hands, either in the ſand or on boards. Others form their figures, letters, words, and ſentences, on paper.

ſave

save the lives of the whole. But kind Providence saved him from that fate, and us from that fatal deed.

At last the wished-for morning came, and about eight o'clock the Havaldar was announced. Our emotions were now wrought up to the highest point of anxiety and suspence. The Havaldar, coming forward into the prison-yard, called out for the insane gentleman. The question on which our safety or our destruction now hung in suspence, was, Is the insane person to be carried before the Keeladar or no? Our joy was extreme when we heard the Havaldar tell him, that if he had any thing to say, the Keeladar had ordered that he should mention it to him. Yet still there was reason to apprehend that he might make such discoveries as the Havaldar could not pass over, though he was naturally humane, had taken a present, and was inclined to save us. We therefore, during the conversation which he held with the Havaldar, crowded around him, spoke in a threatening tone of voice, used menacing looks and gestures,

gestures, and did every thing to embarrass him, and excite his madness. To the Havaldar, who repeatedly put the question, What have you to discover? he constantly replied, that he would not reveal it but to the Havaldar, and poured forth at the same time indefinite reproaches of murderous intentions towards himself against his fellow-prisoners. The Havaldar then told him that he was a fool, and desired that he would go about his business, meaning that he should retire to his cell.

We then requested of the Havaldar, that when he should be relieved, he would report to the commanding officer who should succeed him, the insanity of our fellow-prisoner. If we had used this precaution at first, we might have avoided this dreadful scene. But we had compassion on the infirmity of this poor man, which was brought on by long confinement, lowness of spirits, and the melancholy prospect of death, or perpetual slavery.

We

We felt as much joy at being freed from this dangerous embarraſſment, as if we had been ſet at entire liberty. The inſane perſon had in his poſſeſſion copies of many letters, with papers, knives, and other contraband things. Theſe we wiſhed above all things to get out of his hands. And, after this violent fit of inſanity, he fortunately recovered ſo far, in the courſe of a few days, as to be reaſoned into the propriety of giving up or deſtroying theſe ſuſpicious articles. He behaved pretty well during the remainder of our confinement. He is now on half-pay.

A current report that peace is broken off, and that our ambaſſadors have embarked for Tellicherry.

Raiſed by public ſubſcription twenty-eight fanams, which we have ſent by a truſty hand to our good friend Sid Abram.

Sid Abram acknowledges the receipt of the money, and is very thankful.

1784. For thefe four preceding nights, many black prifoners have been murdered, and a report at prefent prevails, that they intend vifiting our prifon for the fame end,

We are informed that the draught which was adminiftered to General Matthews's officers, to the number of twenty, was the milk of the cocoa-tree. We learned afterwards, from undoubted authority, that Lieutenant Mathews of the Bengal eftablifhment, brother to General Mathews, and Lieutenant Weldon of the Bombay eftablifhment, were, by orders of Tippoo, taken out of the fort at Bednore, at ten o'clock at night, carried to the Jungul, a place over-grown with long grafs and underwood, and there cut to pieces: of which the officers confined at Bednore received the moft certain accounts the next morning, when the clothes of thefe unfortunate victims were brought to them for fale. Directions had in fact been fent by the Sultan to murder all the Englifh officers in the different prifons in his dominions, who would not enter into his fervice: but intelligence

ligence being received that the commissioners for negotiating the treaty of peace had set out for Madras, these bloody orders were countermanded,

1784.

The following is a list of the officers who were poisoned with General Mathews.

King's Officers.

Captain Dougald Campbell, of the 98th regiment.
Captain Alston, of the 100th regiment.
Captain Fish, ditto.
Mr. Gifford, surgeon's assistant, ditto.

Company's Establishment at Bombay.

Brigadier-General Mathews.
Lieutenant Young, Brigade-major.
Major Fewtrill.
Captain Clift.
Captain Gottick.
Lieutenant Barnwell.
Captain Jackson, artillery.
Lieutenant Olivier, ditto.
Captain Richardson, 3d battalion Sepoys.

Captain

1784. Captain Eames, 5th battalion Sepoys.
Captain Lendrum, 11th ditto.
Captain M'Culloch, 15th ditto.
Charles Stewart, Efq; Commiffary.
Charles Cheek, Efq; deputy ditto.

From the foldiers prifon.

" On the 27th October the Keeladar fent
" for Vankatachelliem, our linguift, and told
" him to acquaint us all that the Nabob
" and Company had made peace, and that
" we would foon be fent to Madras. The
" whole of us at that time were hand-cuf-
" fed two and two together. Soon after the
" Keeladar came into the prifon, and or-
" dered the hand-cuffs to be taken off. We
" were fhut up together at that time about
" twelve o'clock at night, and remained fo
" forty days. About four months ago in the
" dead of night, we received the fecond alarm
" of that kind. We were hand-cuffed fingly,
" both hands, fince which the Bramin has
" been four different times to enquire for
" mechanicks, taken all our names down,
" our pay, batta, and rank, in the Com-
" pany's

" pany's service, which makes us all 1784.
" very uneasy, as we cannot imagine
" what they want to do with us: another
" fresh alarm that there has been a num-
" ber of black prisoners taken and massa-
" cred, which is transacted every night.
" We hear that a Commandant and some
" Sepoys belonging to Colonel Braith-
" waite's detachment have suffered the
" above fate."

A letter from Colonel Braithwaite ac- March knowledging the receipt of seventeen fa- 18. nams for the use of Captain Leech.

Sent Captain Leech a supply of eighteen 19. fanams. The Subadars who were confined with him, as also General Mathews's servant, are removed.

Ten o'clock, P. M. visited by the Myar 22. and a Bramin, who ordered Captains Baird, Menteith, and Lindsey's irons to be knocked off. These gentlemen were removed from our prison under the charge of one Havaldar and two Sepoys.

Three

1784.
March 22.

Three o'clock, P. M. the Havaldar returns and acquaints us, that the three gentlemen are at prefent with Colonel Braithwaite: that they were removed to him in confequence of peace, and that we fhould in all probability have our irons knocked off in a day or two, and be fent to Madras. Little credit is given by us to this piece of information, having been fo frequently difappointed before; and we are very uneafy, and apprehenfive that they intend very unfair means with Colonel Braithwaite, and indeed the whole of us, as reports have been current for many days, that Tippoo Saib intends murdering the whole of the European prifoners.

While we were in this gloomy ftate of mind, and ready to fink under the preffure of melancholy and black defpair; behold, within the walls of our difmal dungeon, a Bramin fent from Tippoo Sultan, with a formal intimation of the final conclufion of peace!—And that our irons were to be knocked off next day.—The emotions that fprung up in our breafts on receiving this intelli-

intelligence, were so strong and lively, and raised to such a point of elevation and excess, as almost bordered on pain!—We gave vent to the ardour of our minds in the loudest as well as most irregular and extravagant expressions of congratulations. The whole prison resounded with the frantic voice of sudden as well as excessive joy and exultation. This tumult having in some degree subsided, though we were incapable of entire composure and rest, a proposal was made, and most readily embraced, to collect all the ready money in our possession, without the least regard to equal shares or proportions, and to celebrate the joyful news of our approaching deliverence with some plantain fritters, and sherbet; the only articles of luxury we could then command, on account of our extreme poverty. By nine o'clock at night, supper was announced, consisting of sixty dozen of plantains, and a large chatty of sherbet. Every one being seated on the ground, the repast was received with the utmost content and satisfaction. Friends and toasts were drank, as long as our chatty stood out; and such was the agitation of our minds, that there was not one of us who felt the least

(Vol. 2.) incli-

1784. inclination, or indeed who poffeffed the power to compofe himfelf for fleep. We now waited with the utmoft impatience for the return of day and were impreffed with a ftrong defire that our irons might be knocked off immediately; but, to our great mortification, about feven in the morning, there arrived only one armourer. Every one ftruggled to have his fetters knocked off firft. Promifes, threats, buftling and joftling; every expedient that could be imagined was put in practice, in order to obtain that which would come unfought for, in the courfe of a few minutes, or hours at furtheft. The fame men who had fuffered the rigours of imprifonment, and the menaces of a barbarous policy, with invincible refolution and patience, as well as with mutual fympathy and complaifance, for years, were fo tranfported by the near profpect of liberty, that the delay of a few moments, feemed now to be more infupportable than even the tedious languor of our long, moft alarming, and anxious confinement. Between two and three in the afternoon, our irons were all knocked off, and then we were conducted, under the charge of a guard,

to

to the Keeladar. In crossing the parade to Hyder's palace, several European boys, in the Mahomedan dress, who had been forcibly circumcised, came near to us, imploring our assistance in a most distressful manner. The only consolation we could give them, was, to assure them, that whenever we arrived at Madras, their melancholy situation should be faithfully and feelingly described to the Governor, in order to procure their enlargement. We now were brought before the Keeladar, who was lodged in Hyder's palace, and sat in a veranda, surrounded by his guards. Our names being taken down, with our rank and other circumstances, we were conducted to Colonel Braithwaite's prison, where we found the Colonel, Captains Baird, Lindsey, Menteith, and Ensign Holmes: here we remained several hours, and were, in a most friendly manner, supplied by these gentlemen with money, which gave us an opportunity of rewarding those good men who had at different times been on our guard. Towards the close of the evening, after the soldiers and black prisoners were collected, we moved off from the fort to Soomner-Pettah, a village distant about two miles.

1784. miles. On our arrival at the Choultry of this place, we had an opportunity of conversing with our soldiers. Their marks of affection, respect, and joy, at meeting with their officers, after so long a separation, were not less sincere than extravagant. The sight of the country, the fair face of nature in a rich and delicious climate, from which we had been so long excluded, excited in our minds the most various and pleasing emotions, and struck us with all the force of novelty. At the same time, it may not be thought unimportant to observe, that we had lost, in some degree, that intuitive discernment of the magnitude and relations of objects, which is the effect of experience, habit, and the association of ideas. At Soomner Pettah we were indulged with permission to walk about in the Buzar, and to bathe in the river, a most delicious as well as salutary refreshment. Every object, and every recreation, became now a source of exquisite satisfaction and delight; all that satiety, and indifference to the bounty of nature, which arises from undisturbed possession, and perhaps still more from vicious habits, being effectually overcome and destroyed by the painful purification of months, added

to

to months, in a succession that threatened 1784. to terminate either in perpetual slavery or death.

Having received no allowance of rice, or the three pice, for the preceding day, we asked for some victuals; and some hours after, a seer of rice, and three pice, was delivered to each person. We were amazed, and did not know how to account for the neglect of our pittance; for as peace was concluded, we naturally imagined our allowance would rather have been augmented than curtailed; but on making enquiry into the cause, we were told that the commissioners of Madras, employed in negotiating the treaty, had stipulated no kind of provision for us; and that the Nabob had sent orders to furnish us with just as much as would keep us from starving, and no more.

March 25.

Though our irons were knocked off, it was a long time before we recovered the entire use of our limbs, and learned to walk with perfect freedom: never was the inveterate power of habit more forcibly displayed

1784. played than on this occasion. We could never get the idea of our being in fetters out of our heads. No effort of our minds, no act of volition, could, for several days, overcome the habit of making the short and constrained steps to which we had been so long accustomed. Our crippled manner of walking was a subject of laughter to ourselves as well as to others.

March 25.
On the 25th of March, doolies having been provided for the sick, and a few bad horses, we began our march to Vellore, the place agreed on by the treaty for the delivering up of the British prisoners, guarded by an escort of one hundred cavalry and five hundred infantry, under the command of a native commandant.

April 15.
On the 15th of April we arrived at Oofcottah, a fortress situated eighteen miles eastward of Bangalore, and sixty miles distant from the pass into the Carnatic. Here the whole of the British prisoners, who had been taken at the battle of Tricoallum, or of Perambaukum near Conjeveram, and at Bednore,

Bednore, were assembled together. Their number amounted nearly to one hundred and eighty officers, nine hundred European soldiers, and sixteen hundred Sepoys, besides some hundreds of servants of different castes and occupations. The officers who had been confined at Bangalore, having received frequent supplies of cash from Madras, had it in their power to supply us, as well as the gentlemen from Bednore, with many articles of which we stood greatly in need. This many of them did, sharing their clothes and money with such of their brother-officers and fellow-soldiers as most wanted their assistance.

1784.

On communicating to each other our respective sufferings, it appeared that the officers who were left wounded at Bednore, were much better used than at any other place. They were permitted to keep all their clothes, doolies, cots, chairs, tables, knives, forks, and other articles. They were indulged with the free use of pen, ink, and paper. A certain part of the rampart, including two towers, was given up to them,

1784. them, in which they were at liberty to range about at pleasure. Their servants were permitted to go into the Buzar to purchase whatever they chose to send for, though their daily allowance was only one seer of rice, and one pice to each. They were allowed a French surgeon to attend them; and when they recovered of their wounds they were not put in irons.

Ensign Manly, of the Bombay establishment, who had been taken in a sally at Mangalore, was sent to Bednore, and there confined in the same prison with some Sepoys, with no other allowance than one pice per day, and a seer of raggee.

The officers who were confined at Darwaur, a fort near Goa, were lodged with the private men, upon the same allowance with the other officers who were in prison at Bednore: but they were afterwards removed to Simoga, where they were kept on a seer of raggee and one pice each a day. Their irons were connected together by a straight bar, in such a manner that the unfortunate

unfortunate prisoners could neither expand their legs nor contract them:

The gentlemen confined at Bangalore were not only permitted to purchase every article they wanted, but, during the latter part of their confinement, they were allowed to visit each other in their different prisons. The private Europeans also received different treatment, in the different parts of the country in which they were imprisoned.— The Sepoys were treated with equal severity every where.

Four days before the British officers were removed from Bednore, all the Commandants, Subadars, and Jemmidars, of the Bombay establishment, who had been taken prisoners by Tippoo Sultan Bahadar, were, by his orders, removed from thence, and have not since been heard of. It is but too easy to conjecture the fate of those unfortunate men, when we reflect that he had repeatedly threatened to put them to death for refusing to enter into his service, and on the melancholy examples exhibited of the certainty

1784. tainty and rigour with which his bloody menaces were carried into execution*.

April 17.
Lieutenant Dallas, who had been appointed by the commissioners for peace to receive the prisoners, with a detachment of the Madras cavalry, and two companies of Sepoys, dismounting his horsemen, and supplying as many officers as he could with horses, the whole of the prisoners, escorted by a small guard of the Sultan's, began their march towards Vellore, at which place we all of us arrived on the 25th of April, 1784. Beem Row, a Bramin, whom Tippoo Sultan had appointed to conduct the prisoners from Oofcottah to the confines of the Carnatic, received from Mr. Dallas a receipt for all the prisoners whom the Sultan had delivered up. On this, we were restored to liberty, the value of which we had been taught to estimate by a long and painful confinement.

We look back, now, to the days of our captivity, with a kind of melancholy satis-

* For an account of the situation and sufferings of the prisoners at Bēdnōre, before their arrival at Oofcottah, see Appendix, B.

faction, composed of a thousand mixed emotions not to be described: but which are always deeply tinctured with admiration and gratitude to Mr. Hastings, to whose magnanimous exertions we were indebted for our restoration to liberty, and preservation from death, and the reports of whose transcendent talents and virtues, gloriously displayed under accumulated difficulties, now and then diffused a gleam of hope through the horrors of hard confinement.

Our situation, in prison among the barbarians, is recalled to our remembrance in a lively and accurate manner, by a song that was made by Lieutenant Thewlis, a very engaging and accomplished youth, now, alas! deceased, confined with us in one of the jails of Seringapatam, as also by a poem composed on the prospect of liberty, by an officer under confinement at Bangalore. These pieces, with a statement of some particulars relative to the mode and expence of living in jail among our late enemies in the peninsula of Hindostan, and a view of our prison in Seringapatam, are subjoined to this journal in an appendix.

APPEN-

APPENDIX.

A.

*A Description of an Eastern Haram.
By an English Officer.*

As the subject of the eastern Harams naturally excites curiosity in Europeans, the author of this journal may, perhaps, gratify some of his readers by the following story, of the truth of which he is perfectly certain: although, the parties concerned in it being still alive, it would be improper to mention names, or to be particular as to dates or places.

On the conclusion of the late war in India, a certain officer appointed to collect the revenue in a district dependent on the Company, became acquainted with the Governor

APPENDIX.

Governor or head-man of a town and territory belonging to it, who held that station in the name of the sovereign prince, whose court was established in another part of the country. This delegated power he had swayed for a long course of years, with advantage indeed to himself, but without oppressing the people. A report had been spread that he had become exorbitantly rich: in consequence of which, the prince his master, agreeably to the manner of eastern despots, recalled him from his government to the city where he had fixed his throne, that he might plunder him of the wealth which he had acquired among his distant subjects.

The Governor, having received orders to return home, was struck with all those apprehensions which trouble and distract the deputies of Asiatic chiefs and princes in similar situations. To conciliate the favour of the tyrant by presents, to pacify him by a liberal share of the spoil, is the measure which prudence naturally dictates to the viceroy, who cannot appeal

1784. to any other law than the will of his sovereign. But nothing less than the whole is commonly found sufficient to gratify the rapacity of the prince himself, or those that are about his person. Nay the whole is not always enough to redeem the possessor from imprisonment, torture, and death. For fame exaggerates the utmost amount of his fortune. The more he gives, the greater the store is supposed to be from which he gives it. A considerable hoard is still thought to remain: and, in order to wrest this imaginary treasure from the hands of the miserable owner, every instrument of terror is employed that cruel ingeniousness can devise.

The person whose history has given occasion, at present, to these observations, was fully aware of the extreme danger of his situation; and, in the anxiety of his mind, communicated what had happened to him to the English officer above-mentioned. This gentleman, touched with his distresses, and sensible that he would risque all that was desirable or dear to man,

if

if he should return to his master; undertook to represent his case to the presidency of ————, and at the same time to make them fully sensible how well he deserved of the English, to whose interests, indeed, he had shewn an uniform attachment. This the officer did without delay, and comforted the Governor with the hope of the Company's protection. This was, in fact, readily granted. The Governor was invited within the boundaries of the presidency's jurisdiction, with assurances of perfect security to his property, and safety to his person.

Upon this he moved off with his family, his furniture, and his wealth, carried on a number of elephants, to the town of ————, where he now resides.

To the officer who had been the means of procuring him this asylum, he was anxious to shew his gratitude by all possible marks of affection, esteem, and confidence. He declared, that, notwithstanding the difference of their religions, he could not help considering the officer as of kin to his family, ly, of which, under God, *the common Father of mankind,* (that was his expreſſion) he had been the Saviour. As the utmoſt mark of confidence and favour he could beſtow, he invited the Engliſh gentleman to his Haram, that he might preſent him to his wives and family. The gentleman was very well pleaſed with this invitation: but he obſerved, ſmiling, that this favour would be a treſpaſs againſt the laws and cuſtoms of his religion, which was the Mahomedan. The generous Muſſulman ſaid, that there was no reaſon why all the world ſhould be made acquainted with what paſſed between them: and, for the act itſelf, if he conſidered it as a deviation from duty in any degree, he ſeemed to think it a very venial and light one.

Upon a certain day, then, at an appointed hour in the forenoon, the officer went to viſit his friend, who received him in a large veſtibule, attended by a numerous train of ſervants. He was conducted, by a ſpacious and elegant ſtair-caſe, to a gallery that led to the women's apartments, called the *Haram,*

APPENDIX.

ram, and alfo, in the Gentoo language, the *Zenana*, which look into a fpacious garden, where the ladies occafionally take the benefit of the frefh air, enclofed with high walls. In certain apartments, at either end of this gallery, there were feveral females whofe bufinefs it was to wait on the ladies of the Haram. As foon as the Englifh officer entered within the hall, or what refembled a fpacious drawing room, the whole of the ladies rofe up from the rich carpet on which they reclined on cufhions of the fineft crimfon velvet, and inclining their heads towards the ground, paid him the compliment of the falam with inexpreffible benignity and grace. Four of thefe ladies, diftinguifhed by the richnefs of their apparel, and the eafe and dignity of their mien, were in the rank of wives; one of whom feemed to exercife a fpecies of authority, to which the others paid a ready and cheerful deference. The other girls, to the number of ten or twelve, ferved as concubines to their mafter, and in fome refpects as handmaids to their miftreffes.— They were all of them, thofe efpecially who were in the honoured rank of wives, and

descended

descended from good families, very great beauties. They were well dressed and highly perfumed: but the exquisite comeliness and elegance of the wives was set off and heightened with costly jewels, which adorned their ears and necks, and arms and ancles, and were stuck in their thick and long black hair, which was braided and turned back in the most graceful manner.

They were aware that this stranger was to be introduced. They had been informed of what he had done for the family, and it was, perhaps, in compliance with their solicitations that he was admitted to their apartments: for, like other females, as afterwards appeared, they possessed great curiosity; and they had never, probably, seen, and certainly never before been present and conversed with a native of Europe; yet, they were not in the least abashed or constrained in their deportment. They were perfectly at their ease, and behaved with great attention and complaisance to the Englishman, as well as with complacency towards each other. They invited him, after
he

he was feated on a kind of low fopha, to partake of a collation, confifting of various delicacies, prefented from time to time by female flaves, who did not feem to be under the influence of any fear or awe, but were, on the contray, as well as the ladies who were their miftreffes, though refpectful and fubmiffive, unconftrained and cheerful.

The ladies of the Haram, and efpecially thofe in the rank of wives, were very inquifitive concerning the people, the cuftoms, and manners of the Feringees* ; and efpecially of the Feringee ladies. One of them afked if England was a large country, and how many gates it had. This was a natural enough queftion: for what could fhe reafon but from what fhe knew? The only fpot of ground with which fhe was at all acquainted, was the garden adjoining to the Haram, or, at moft, the town in which fhe had formerly, or that in which fhe now refided.

* White people, or Europeans.

Another

APPENDIX.

Another asked him, if it was true that the ladies in his country went openly in the streets, and into the mosques, without veils, and in the company of the men: and another, whether the men were confined, by the law, to one wife. Many other questions were put concerning European manners and customs. The answers that were given to these by the English officer, appeared so improbable to the ladies, that one of them, who seemed either to possess, or to affect greater penetration than the rest, whispered to one that stood by her, that she was afraid that their *protector*, the title with which they honoured the gentleman, was telling a story.

The master of the House, the common husband of all the ladies, who sat by them all the while smoaking his hooker, laughed very heartily both at their curiosity and their unbelief.

It is easy to conjecture that the wives and concubines of this Mahomedan chief were not so much distinguished as many of our
English

English ladies, by a taste and proficiency in literature. Many of the higher ranks among the Moors, even princes and princesses, can neither read nor write. Yet they cannot be said to be wholly uncultivated by letters. Their servants or slaves, both male and female, instructed in the arts of reading, writing, and arithmetic, supply the want of these accomplishments to their lords and ladies, too indolent, or barbarously proud, to submit themselves to any occupation that bears the semblance of application and trouble. The ladies of the Haram that is the subject of these notes, I understood, on enquiry, were frequently entertained by songs, and most extravagant tales, in the oriental manner, such as the Arabian Nights Entertainments, read to them by their handmaidens. In this country the system of the late Lord Chesterfield, who considered it as below a gentleman to practise on any musical instrument, is carried to its full extent and completion: for there the fine gentlemen and ladies avoid the labour of musical execution, and of arts and sciences of every kind.

As

1784. As the Hindoo ladies receive the benefit of books without the faculty of reading, so they also enjoy the pleasures of music and dancing, without the trouble of taking an active part in either. I wonder, says an Hindoo to an European who walks a minuet at a ball, that you should take the trouble to dance, when you have, or may have, so many servants to dance for you. Climate influences every human passion, disposition and sentiment, nay, and perhaps some of our speculative and most abstracted opinions. The Supreme Being, according to the Platonic philosophy, the product of an indolent climate, acted by a *Demiurgus*. And in Earth, as well as in Heaven, every thing, under an enervating climate, is done by deputation. It is to climate, and that despotism to which climate gives birth, that we are to trace those ideas of predestination and irresistible fate which prevail in Asia, and prepare the mind for an acquiescence in all events. Hence death is regarded with less horror in India than in any other country in the world. The origin and the end of all things, according to

the

APPENDIX.

the philosophers of India, is a *vacuum*.—
A state of repose is the state of greatest perfection: and this is the state after which a wise man aspires. It is better, say the Hindoos, to sit than to walk, and to sleep than to wake; but death is the best of all.

It is no wonder, then, that the ladies of the Zenana chuse to be spectators rather than actresses' in the operas exhibited for their entertainment. Balladieres, or dancing girls, a class of females who are allowed to be openly prostituted, are generally entertained in wealthy families, for the amusement of the women. The attitudes, as well as the movements of the Balladieres, are very easy and not ungraceful. Their persons are delicately formed, gaudily attired, and highly perfumed. By the continuation of wanton attitudes, they acquire, as they grow warm in the dance, a frantic lasciviousness themselves, and communicate, by a natural contagion, the most voluptuous desires to the beholders.

The Hindoos, as well as the Persians, Tartars, and adjoining nations, who have inhabited Hindostan since it was conquered by Tamerlane, or Timurbeg, though of different nations, religions, laws, and customs, possess nevertheless, in equal degrees, hospitality, politeness and address. In refinement and ease, they are superior to any people to the westward of them. In politeness and address, in gracefulness of deportment, and speech, an Hindoo is as much superior to a Frenchman of fashion, as a French courtier is to a Dutch burgo-master. A Frenchman is indeed by no means deficient in ease of carriage; but that ease is mixed with forward familiarity, with confidence, and self-conceit. The Hindoos, especially those of the higher *Castes*, are in their demeanour easy and unconstrained, still more than even a French courtier; but their ease and freedom is reserved, modest, and respectful. A Frenchman is polite because he thinks it his honour to be polite: an Indian, because he thinks it his duty. The former is polite because he regards himself; the latter because he respects you.

Their

Their perfons are ftraight and elegant, their limbs finely proportioned, their fingers long and tapering, their countenances open and pleafant, and their features exhibit the moft delicate lines of beauty in the females, and in the males a kind of manly foftnefs. Their walk and gait, as well as their whole deportment, is in the higheft degree graceful. The drefs of the men is a kind of clofe-bodied gown, like our women's gowns, and wide trowfers, refembling petticoats, reaching down to their flippers. Such of the women as appear in public, have fhawls over their heads and fhoulders, exactly fuch garments, and worn in fuch a manner, as the Scotch plaids, fhort clofe jackets, and tight drawers which come down to their ancles. Hence the drefs of the men gives them, in the eyes of Europeans, an appearance of effeminacy; whereas that of the women will appear rather mafculine: fuch is the influence of habit and cuftom on human fentiments; an influence which extends not merely to matters of tafte, but, as the ingenious Dr. Smith, in his *Theory of Moral Sentiments*, obferves, to objects of higher importance.

From the difference of Caftes or claffes of the people in Hindoftan, I mean the original inhabitants, there arifes a difference of education and drefs. But even the inferior claffes are taught reading, writing, and arithmetic: the youth are taught, not within doors, but in the open air; and it is a fingular, but not unpleafing fpectacle, to behold, in every village, a venerable old man, reclined on a terraced plain, teaching a number of furrounding boys, who regard him with the utmoft reverence and attention, like a fhepherd feeding his flock. In thofe fimple feminaries, where the want of magnificient halls and theatres is *divinely* compenfated by the fpacious canopy of Heaven, the gentle and tractable fons of the Hindoos are not only prepared for the bufinefs, but inftructed in the duties of life; a profound veneration for the object or objects of religious worfhip; reverence of their parents; refpect for their feniors; juftice and humanity towards all men, but a particular affection for thofe of their own *Cafte*.

The

APPENDIX.

The Hindoo language is beautiful, expressive, and nervous. In reading and speaking, the Hindoos are very mufical. Their speech, like that of the Italians, flows in a kind of numbers. There is a dead language, underftood only by the *literati* of the country, that is, the priefts, called the *Sanfcrit* language, in which their facred volumes are written, even as our facred fcriptures are written in Greek and Hebrew. But whether that language was originally different from that of the country, or whether it has only *now* become unintelligible to the people, through that change which is incident to all living languages, is, I believe, not well known.

Having already obferved, that the genius of the Hindoos is rather imitative than inventive, I need fcarcely add, that they have lefs curiofity in their nature than the European nations have; that they do not vary their fafhions; and that they are not fond of novelty *beyond the precincts of their Harams*. From the temper and tenets of this people, as well as from feveral hints in ancient

cient hiftorians, it appears more than probable, that the fame kind of garments, of food, of furniture, of buildings, and of manners, which obtained among their progenitors thoufands of years ago, actually prevails among the Hindoo tribes at this day. In like manner, the fame profeffions are adhered to by the fame families with fuperftitious exactnefs. Thofe profeffions are exceedingly numerous. This divifion and fubdivifion of employment and labour; the vaft variety of caftes, from the *Bramins* down to the fifherman, is one proof, among many others, of the antiquity of the Hindoo nation, and their progrefs in the arts. It appears very fingular, that the different caftes are not only prohibited from intermarrying, but alfo from eating with one another, and, in fome inftances, even from eating of the fame kind of food.

The food of the Hindoos is fimple, confifting chiefly of rice, ghee, which is a kind of imperfect butter, milk, vegetables, and oriental fpices of different kinds, but chiefly what is called in the eaft, *chilly*, and in the weft, west, green or cayenne pepper. The warrior *caste* may eat of the flesh of goats, mutton, and poultry, which is dressed into *carryes* and *pilaws* *. Other superior castes may eat poultry and fish; but the inferior castes are prohibited from eating flesh or fish of any kind. Their greatest luxury consists in the use of the richest spiceries and perfumes, of which the great people are very lavish. Their dress, in point of richness, is proportioned to their stations: their pomp and equipage consist in a numerous retinue of servants of various denominations, who attend all their visits and excursions; in the dresses of those attendants; the elegance of their palanquins; and the caparisons of their horses, camels, and elephants.

* *Carryes* are a kind of *fricassees* of mutton, fowl, or fish; the sauce of which is composed of dried vegetables, peculiar to the east, and fine rice, boiled with very little water, introduced on a separate plate: The sauce of the fricassee is poured on the rice, and the meat laid above both. The *pilaw* is fine Patna rice dry-boiled, and fried with *ghee*, which has been already described, mixed with various spices, and particularly the *cardamon*, brought in on a large dish, in which is concealed, amidst the rice, a boiled fowl, or part of a kid, or of a lamb.

It is superfluous to observe, that in consequence of this multiplicity of different ranks, the Hindoos have the highest ideas of subordination, and pay to their superiors the same ready deference and homage, which they expect themselves from their inferiors.

Their houses cover much ground, and have spacious galleries and accommodations of various kinds. The apartments are small, and the furniture not very elegant, if we except the richest Persian carpets. The grandeur of their palaces consists in baths, perfumes, temples, gods, and harams. The *harams* are removed from the front of the house, and lighted either from a square space in the centre of the whole building, or from a garden behind, enclosed by thick and high walls, fortified, sometimes, with bastions. The apparel of the women is inconceivably rich; they have jewels on their fingers and about their necks, and also in their ears and nostrils, with bracelets not only on their wrists, but on their arms above their elbows, and on their legs around their ancles.

Although

Although the Hindoos are naturally the most inoffensive of all mortals, yet does their humanity consist more in abstaining from injurious, than in the performance of beneficent actions. There is a wonderful mildness in their manners, and also in their laws, which are influenced by their manners; by which the murder of an human creature, and of a cow, are the only crimes that are punished by death. Yet with all this gentleness of disposition, they are inferior to the boisterous Europeans, with all their vices, in the virtues of compassion and generosity. They are wanting in that tenderness which is the most amiable part of our nature.—They are less affected by the distresses and dangers, and even the accidental deaths of one another, than any nation in the old or new world. Yet they *love* to excess: a proof, either of the inconsistency of the human character; or that the amorous passion is not derived from the noblest part of our nature.

Although the practice of Hindoo women burning themselves on the funeral piles of their husbands, and embracing in the mean time

time their dead bodies in their arms, be not so general now as it has formerly been, yet does it still prevail among some of the wives of men of high caste and condition: and although this effort of frantic love, courage, and ambition, be deemed an aggrandizement of the family and relations of both husband and wife, but especially of the wife's, yet their friends and relations constantly endeavour to dissuade the women who declare their resolutions of *burning*, from carrying them into execution. Even the *Bramins* do not encourage this practice.

The causes which inspire Hindoo women with this desperate resolution, are the following:

In the first place; as the wife has from her earliest infancy been betrothed in marriage to her husband, and from that time has never been permitted to see another man; as she is instructed to believe that he is perfectly accomplished, and taught to respect and honour him; as, after consummation, she is shut up from the company, conversation, and even the sight of other men,

men, with still greater care, if possible, than before, being now debarred from seeing even the father or elder brother of her husband, the bonds of her affection must needs be inconceivably strong and indissoluble. To an European lady, the Zenana naturally appears in the light of an horrible prison: but the daughters of Asia never consider confinement to the Zenana as any hardship. They consider it as a condition of their existence, and they enjoy all the happiness of which they have any conception; their whole desires being concentered and fixed on their husband, their children, their food, jewels, and female attendants.— There are instances of women making elopements from the Harams with European gentlemen. But these are not, in general, of the first families; nor free from the imputation of loose behaviour.

'In the second place, if the wife survive her husband, she cannot marry again, and is treated as an inferior person, and an outcast from her family. Nay, she is obliged, in her mournful and hopeless widow-hood, to perform all the offices of a menial servant.

In

In the third place, she is flattered with the idea of having immortalized her name, and aggrandized her children, and her own and husband's families.

Lastly, she is rendered insensible to the pains and horrors of what she is to suffer, by those intoxicating perfumes and mixtures which are administered to her after she has declared her final and unalterable resolution—I say her final resolution, because one or two declarations, of an intention to die with her husband, is not sufficient. The strength of her resolution undergoes a probation.— There is a certain time prescribed by the Gentoo law, during which her family and friends exert their utmost influence, in order to dissuade her from burning; and if she persist in her resolution to the end of that period, it is not lawful to use any more persuasions with her, to abandon it. If she should alter her purpose after that period, she would be punished with the loss of all *castes*, and live in a state of the most complete misery and contempt. Nay, if an European or Christian does but touch her very

APPENDIX.

very garment with his finger, when she is going to the pile, an immediate stop is put to the ceremony, she is forced to live an outcast from her family, and from the Gentoo religion.

It is a natural object of curiosity to know, in what manner, after all these stimulatives to perseverance, the tender sex, among a soft and effeminate people, sustains the near approach of a scene so full of awe and horror. Amidst her weeping relations and friends, the voluntary victim to love and honor alone appears serene and undaunted. A gentle smile is diffused over her countenance: she walks upright, with an easy but firm step; talks to those around her of the virtues of the deceased, and of the joy with which she will be transported when her shade shall meet with his; and encourages her sorrowful attendants to bear with fortitude the *sight* of those momentary sufferings which she herself is about to *feel*. Having ascended the funeral pile, she lays herself down by the body of her husband, which she fervently embraces.—

A

A dose of narcotic mixtures is then administered for the last time; and instantly the person, whose office it is, sets fire to the pile.

Thus the most determined resolution of which we can form any conception, is found in the weaker sex, and in the soft climes of Asia. It is to the honour of that sex and those climes, that the greatest courage they exhibit, is the effect, not of the furious impulses of rage and revenge, but conscious dignity and love.

It might naturally be imagined by an European, that the several wives of one man, for polygamy is general throughout all Asia, would regard one another with mutual jealousy and aversion; and that they in reality do, has been asserted by writers of high reputation. The fact however is quite otherwise: though each has her own separate apartment, they visit one another with great friendship and cordiality; and if they are of the same *caste*, will occasionally eat together. The husband is sometimes restrained reftrained from eating with his wives, either by a regard to cuftom; or, as I have been informed by fome of the Gentoos themfelves, by a precept of their religion.

Thefe obfervations, fome of which are applicable only to thofe of the Gentoo religion, are indeed a digreffion from the prefent fubject: but without a notion of certain general cuftoms and fentiments, common to all, it would be difficult to form a juft conception of any particular Haram. With refpect to the Haram that was vifited in the capital of one of our Eaft-India fettlements by an Englifh officer, I have only to add, that the children of his friend were prefented to him, as well as his ladies, and that, at his departure, he was complimented with a diamond ring by one of them, who feemed to be the moft favoured and refpected Sultana, and with a moft graceful and benign falam from the whole. The mafter of the houfe obferved, with a fmile, that he repofed perfect confidence in the gentleman's difcretion.

APPENDIX.

B.

A Narrative of the Treatment of the English Prisoners taken at Bednore, by the Nawaub Tippoo Sultaun Bahauder, on the 28th of March, 1783. By an Officer.

THE siege of Bednore having lasted seventeen days, a cessation of arms took place on the 24th of April, 1783, and, on the 26th of the same month, Brigadier-General Richard Mathews, commander in chief of the forces on the western side of India, called a council of war, who, after deliberating on the situation of affairs, came to a resolution of capitulating on the following terms, viz.

" That

"That the garrison should march out of
"the fort with the honours of war, and
"pile their arms on the glacis: That all
"public stores should remain in the fort:
"That all prisoners taken since the siege
"began should be delivered up: That, after
"being joined by the garrisons of Cowla-
"droog and Annantpore (who were includ-
"ed in these articles) the whole should have
"full liberty to march, unmolested, with all
"their private property, to Sadashagur, from
"thence to embark for Bombay: That
"Tippoo Sultaun Nawaub Bahauder should
"furnish a guard to march with the English
"troops, for their protection through the
"country, which guard should be under
"the orders of Brigadier-General Mathews:
"That Tippoo Sultaun Nawaub Bahauder,
"should likewise furnish the English troops
"with a plentiful bazar, and proper convey-
"ances for the sick and wounded, during their
"march to Sadashagur: That a guard of
"one hundred Sepoys, from the garrison of
"Bednore, with their arms and accoutre-
"ments, and thirty-six rounds of ammuni-
"tion, should attend Brigadier-General Ma-
"thews

" thews as a body-guard, during the march
" to Sadafhagur; and that Tippo Sultaun
" Nawaub Bahauder, for the performance
" of the articles on his part, fhould deliver
" two hoftages prior to the garrifon's march-
" ing out of the fort."

The capitulation having been figned, the hoftages received, and doolies fent for the fick and wounded, the garrifon marched out of the fort, with the honours of war, on the 28th of April, 1783; and, after piling their arms on the glacis, were immediately efcorted by a ftrong body of the enemy to a tank about half a mile beyond the Onore Gate, where the General was informed he muft encamp that night, to which he reluctantly confented, it being his intention to have marched two miles further. When the whole came up, the enemy furrounded us, and pofted fentries on every fide, beyond whom no perfon was permitted to pafs. The General calling for his body-guard, was informed, that the enemy had forcibly taken away their arms and ammunition immediately on their leaving the fort, and had also

also deprived many of the officers of their side arms. Lieutenant M'Kenzie of the 100th, who had a few days before been shot through the breast, was forced out of his dooly by the enemy, with their bayonets, as he was coming out of the fort, and several others were treated in the like cruel manner. Captain Facey, of the Bombay establishment, with fifty sick and wounded, were detained in the fort till next morning, with Mr. Shields, assistant-surgeon, which latter gentleman informed us, that an Englishman in the Nawaub's service had taken an opportunity of telling him, he was extremely sorry to see him and his fellow-sufferers in so miserable a situation: that there was not the smallest hope of ever being given up, or of getting away; as the Nawaub had employed several artificers in forging irons for the garrison, ever since his arrival before Bednore; and that he himself had been taken and used in the same manner in the Carnatic, after the troops had capitulated.

Early in the morning, while we were preparing to march, the General received a message from the Nawaub, defiring to fee him, together with Captains Eames and Lendrum, of the Bombay eftablifhment, and Mr. Charles Stewart the paymafter. He accordingly went, accompanied by thofe gentlemen, and carried feveral of the officers fervants along with him, in hopes of recovering thofe articles of which they had been plundered. Soon after their departure, a good bazar, furnifhed with a great variety of provifions and other articles, arrived in camp: at the fame time people came to carry away the doolies, out of which they threw the fick and wounded in a moft inhuman manner, dragging thofe who had lately fuffered amputation by the ftumps, and leaving them in that painful wretched condition upon the bare ground, entirely expofed to the heat of the fun. Being afked the caufe of fuch barbarous ufage, the inhuman wretches replied with the moft infulting indifference, "We have received "orders to make the doolies two feet long- "er." The troops had waited with the greateft greateſt impatience for the General's return till five o'clock in the evening, when intelligence was received, that the General, and the gentlemen who accompanied him, were, immediately on their arrival at the Durbar, (without being admitted into the Nawaub's preſence) made cloſe priſoners. While we were lamenting the miſerable proſpect held out to us by theſe melancholy tidings, and waiting the iſſue in a ſtate of the utmoſt anxiety, we were alarmed by the arrival of an additional force of the enemy, when the guards turned out and poſted double ſentries all round us; their deſign was eaſily ſeen through, though they endeavoured to lull our ſuſpicions with the pretext, that thoſe guards which had been firſt placed over us, were a part of Mahomed Ally's troops, who were going to be relieved, in order to be ſent to Mangalore,

The next morning we perceived the enemy had ſent ſpies into every part of our camp, and emiſſaries employed to entice the troops to enter into their ſervice. About ten o'clock, a meſſage was received from the

the Nawaub, defiring to know what number of tents we wanted, at the fame time informing us we were to remain there fome days: the tents we refufed; but a letter, figned by all the officers, was written to the Nawaub, requiring him immediately to fulfil the terms of capitulation. We fent this letter by Major Fewtrill, of the Bombay eftablifhment, who was ordered into Bednore with Captain Alfton, commanding officer of his Majefty's troops, and Lieutenant Younge, Major of Brigade to the Bombay troops; but no anfwer was received.

Early the next morning a report prevailed, that the troops were to be plundered of their property, which we foon found to be true; for at ten o'clock the bazar was taken away, the guards ordered under arms, all the European officers fent for immediately to the fpot of ground from whence the bazar had been removed; where we were, one by one, plundered by the enemy, in the moft rude and fcandalous manner, of our horfes, palanquins, money, plate, watches, and

and other valuables. In fhort we were deprived of every article, except our bedding and clothes, and fearched moft minutely in every part, without the leaft regard to decency: the European foldiers, black officers, and Sepoys, with their wives and children, as alfo all the camp-followers, were fearched and plundered in the fame indecent, infamous manner; and in the afternoon were marched under a ftrong guard to Bednore, leaving the fick and wounded to perifh on the ground: fhortly after the European officers, with their fervants, were likewife conducted to Bednore, where we were clofely confined in the barracks, which had been formerly occupied by a battalion of our own Sepoys; and from the time thefe remorfelefs villains began to fearch and plunder us, we had nothing of any kind to eat, till twelve o'clock the next day, at which time they brought and delivered to each perfon, one pice, and a feer of the coarfeft rice, which they informed us was to be the daily allowance of officers and fervants indifcriminately.

APPENDIX.

On the 5th of the same month, all our servants, except one to each officer, were taken away. The expreſſions of ſorrow which theſe poor creatures ſhewed on this occaſion cannot be eaſily deſcribed; their affection to their maſters, added to the apprehenſions of being led away to death or ſlavery for life, produced the ſtrongeſt emotions of grief; and as we could only lament their fate without affording them the ſmalleſt aſſiſtance, our minds were moſt deeply affected.

On the 6th, the ſubaltern officers belonging to Annantpore, were brought priſoners to the barracks, who informed us of their having ſeen the officers of Cowladroog, and the gariſons of that place and Annantpore, in irons; and alſo, that all the fine young men of the third and fifteenth battalions of Sepoys, were, by order of the Nawaub, forcibly taken away in order to be made ſlaves of, and put into his Cheelah battalions.

On

On the 7th, Lieutenant Morrifon of the 100th regiment, and Lieutenants M'Kenzie and Barnewell, of the Bombay eftablifhment, were brought in chains; the two former gentlemen were taken at Cundapore, the latter at the commencement of the fiege, with Captain Gotlich of the Bombay eftablifhment. Thefe gentlemen informed us, they had been in irons for fome days.— This day we wrote a letter, figned by all the officers prefent, to Lieutenant-Colonel De Coffigné, commanding officer of the French troops, reprefenting to him, in a fpirited manner, the Nawaub's bafe violation of the conditions on which Bednore furrendered, as alfo, his fhameful and cruel conduct towards the troops in general, requefting, in the name of his Britannic Majefty, and the Eaft-India Company, that he would ufe his moft ftrenuous endeavours with the Nawaub, to perfuade him to adhere to the terms of the capitulation, or, if he failed of fuccefs in that point, that he wonld, at leaft, obtain a mitigation of the inhuman and unprecedented ufage we had met with. We contrived to fend this letter by a
French

French officer, who had been taken prisoner by us during the siege, and had come to the barracks, with a surgeon of that nation, to return the civilities he had received from some of our officers, during his confinement. We flattered ourselves with great hope of redress from this letter, particularly as the French officer assured us that Lieutenant-Colonel De Coffigné was very well inclined to exert himself in our cause, and as he gave us his word of honour that he would immediately wait on the Colonel, and deliver him our letter; but, to our utter astonishment and mortification, we never received an answer from Lieutenant-Colonel De Coffigné, nor did any other of the French officers come near us during our stay in the barracks, or offer us the smallest relief in our distressed situation.— The chagrin we felt on this occasion, contributed not a little to encrease the indisposition of many of the officers, who were daily falling sick of fevers and fluxes, which we could only attribute to our wretched food, and the putrid stench arising from the privy.— The French surgeons would afford us no
assistance;

affiftance; our own furgeons had it not in their power, having been plundered of their inftruments and medicines at the time of the general fearch. The fame day Doctor Carmichael of the Bombay eftablifhment, was fent for by the Nawaub, to vifit Brigadier-General Mathews, whom he found much indifpofed; and by whom he was informed, that the Nawaub was endeavouring to intimidate him into a furrender of all the forts in the low country, by threatening to blow him away from a gun, in cafe of his non-compliance.

In the evening the Nawaub was fo generous, as to fend us a prefent of thirty-five fmall fowls and a few falt fifhes, to be divided among upwards of eighty officers.

On the 8th, in the morning, the captains belonging to the garrifons of Cowladroog and Annantpore, together with Captain Gotlich, (who, as before-mentioned, was taken prifoner at the commencement of the fiege) were brought under a guard to the barracks, and were fhortly after removed

ved (with the rest of the captains, Mr. Gifford, Surgeon's-Mate of the 100th regiment, Lieutenants Barnewell and Olivier, of the Bombay establishment, and Mr. Chick, Deputy Commissary) to a separate place of confinement,

On the 9th, we were ordered to prepare to march, and were informed we should not be allowed coolies to carry our baggage; we therefore packed up as much linen as we could well carry ourselves, and giving our bedding to our servants, we all, except Captain Pyne and Ensign Jenour, of the 102d regiment, and Captain Facey, with Lieutenants Williamson, Baird, and Lee, of the Bombay establishment, who were in too desperate a situation, from their wounds, to be removed, went into the street, where we were first stripped of our coats, and then chained two and two, by the hands, three of the officers being linked to private soldiers; after which, we were a second time searched and plundered. We were then secured in another house till about three o'clock in the afternoon, when we we were led through crowds of people, in this ignominious manner, more like criminals going to the place of execution, than Britiſh officers made priſoners contrary to the rules of war, to the enemy's camp, a ſhort diſtance beyond the Delly Gate, where we heard we were to be confined in a ſtrong fort, called Chettledroog. The enemy, at the time we were leaving the barracks, gave us an inſtance of the treatment we might in future expect to receive, in their behaviour to Lieutenant Alexander M'Donald, of the Bombay eſtabliſhment, who was ſo extremely ill that he could ſcarcely ſtand. This gentleman requeſted permiſſion to remain behind with the wounded officers, which they obſtinately refuſed, beating him and dragging him out by the heels : but, to the honour of the French, we were informed that their treatment of Lieutenant Lambert, of the Bombay eſtabliſhment, whom they had taken dangerouſly wounded at the commencement of the ſiege, was full of tenderneſs and humanity.

On

APPENDIX.

On the 10th, in the morning, as we were moving off the ground, each officer received three pice for that day's subsistence. We marched about fifteen miles, and found the apprehensions of yesterday fully justified by this day's usage on the road; several of the gentlemen, who were ill, and much fatigued by the intense heat of the sun, and the want of water, attempting to rest themselves under a tree, were beat in a most unmerciful manner by the enemy, with swords and sticks, while others were driven on with the butts of their firelocks, spit upon, and abused in the grossest manner. Whenever we approached a town or village, four or five men were advanced in the front with horns and tom-toms, that the inhabitants might, by their discordant music, be assembled together to gaze at us as we passed through. We proceeded on in this miserable condition, each day bringing on a renewal of our sufferings, till our arrival at Simoga, a fort on the banks of a river, sixty miles eastward of Bednore, our allowance having been encreased to one fanam each per day, and coolies furnished to carry

carry our bedding and clothes, whenever the commanding officer of the escort thought proper to procure them. As we were to halt here one day, we fondly expected some little indulgences, especially for those gentlemen who were ill; but our inhuman enemy, as if delighted with every fresh opportunity of augmenting our afflictions, when intreated to afford some assistance to Lieutenant Fireworker West, of the Bombay establishment, and Serjeant Dobbins, of the 102d regiment, who had been struck with the sun, owing to our long and severe marches, absolutely refused it, saying, "they "were only drunk," and seemed to exult in their misery, although the one was quite speechless, and the other raving mad: nor were they satisfied with this, but even extended their brutish insults to the lifeless body of Lieutenant Waugh, of the Bombay establishment, whose death was evidently hastened by the injuries he had received upon the road.

On the 14th, we had the misfortune to lose Lieutenant Clements, of the Bombay establishment,

establishment, who, on his departure from Bednore, was in perfect good health, but on the last day's march received a severe stroke of the sun, of which he died, chained to Ensign Gilkie, of the same establishment, who remained in that dreadful situation several hours. In the evening, Lieutenant Sutton, of the Bombay establishment, was seized with the cramp and spasms in his stomach. Lieutenant Reddie, who was hand-cuffed to him, and in great danger of having his arm broke, unriveted his irons by permission of one of the escort, for which he was immediately taken to a tree, and threatened to be hanged, and ropes were prepared for that purpose; the Jemmidar informing us he had received orders to hang every one who should even attempt to free himself from his fetters: but on a submissive representation of the business, Lieutenant Reddie was so far indulged, as to escape with a few lashes only. We again made application for assistance for Lieutenant Sutton, to which we received the following brutal reply, mingled with a large share of eastern abuse: " Let him die, and
" when

" when he is dead we will drag him out of
" the camp by his heels:" however, by
the merciful hand of Providence he recovered in a few hours.

About ten o'clock at night, came on a
moſt violent thunder-ſtorm, which laſted
for ſome hours, and having no kind of ſhelter from the rain, we all ſuffered exceedingly, particularly the ſick, whoſe diſorders
were much increaſed by it. Some of the
gentlemen, who were troubled with ſevere
fluxes and agues, being much affected by
the rain and raw cold wind, went to ſome
fires made by the guard after the ſtorm had
ceaſed, in order to warm themſelves; but
were ſoon given to underſtand that it was
too great an indulgence for Britiſh officers
to enjoy, being inſtantly drove away from
the fires by the enemy, with the butts of
their firelocks.

We left this place on the morning of the
15th, and, after a ſhort march, arrived at
Holly Honoor, a fort ſituated on the eaſt
bank of a rapid river, and, for the firſt time
since

since we began our march, were brought under cover. As the coolies were bringing Ensign Cadogan of the Bombay establishment, who was extremely ill, into the fort, he endeavoured to shift his posture in the quilt in which he was carried, for which he received a blow on the head, and died in a short time afterwards; when he was, in like manner with the former deceased officers, stripped of every article, and in that naked state thrown into an hole by the side of the river, without suffering us to pay our last duty to the deceased. As we approached the destined place of confinement, our escort began to relax a little in their severity, and supplying bullocks to some of the sick to ride on (for the use of which we gave part of the few clothes we had with us) by slow marches we arrived on the 21st of May, 1783, at Chittledroog, a strong and almost impenetrable fortress, irregularly built on the end of a ridge of hills, surrounded by a flat country, one hundred and twenty-eight miles eastward of Bednore. Here we were conducted in triumph to a street leading to the Durbar, where we were surrounded by

crowds

crowds of people, and detained till four o'clock in the afternoon; at which hour all the fervants, except one to every five officers, were taken away; they then divided us into two parties, and marched us up through ten very ftrong gateways, to the top of one of the higheft hills, where we were clofely confined in two feparate houfes; and after having a third time fearched and plundered us, our hand-cuffs were knocked off, and irons put to our legs.— Late in the evening, having had nothing to eat the whole day, they brought us fome rice, with wood and water to drefs it; and next morning we were ordered to deliver up all our knives and papers, but were permitted to keep a few books, which fome of the officers had brought with them: they then furnifhed us with an hand-mill for the purpofe of grinding rice, which afterwards became our chief employment. About ten o'clock a Bramin came up, and delivered to each perfon one feer of the coarfeft rice and two pice, with wood fufficient to cook our victuals, which he told us was to be our daily allowance. Our fervants were allowed ed each a pice a-day. We were alfo furnifhed with a bazar pretty well fupplied with every article except butcher's meat.— We were at this time confined entirely to the two houfes, but informed that a privy was building in the outer yard, to which, when finifhed, we fhould be permitted to go.

On the 29th, this building being compleated, two gentlemen at a time were permitted to go into the outer yard, a fmall area furrounded by an high wall.

On the 4th of June, we fent our compliments to Dowlat Bhauee, the Jemmidar of the province, acquainting him it was our King's birth-day, and on that account requefted we might be allowed fome meat; in confequence of this application, out of his great generofity, he condefcended to order a fmall lean fheep to be delivered to us, for which we paid a moft exorbitant price, and which was but of little fervice to us, as we were forty in number.

On

On the 8th, the wood which had hitherto been ferved to us was ftopped, nor would the enemy fupply us with more, until we confented to pay for it, which additional expence deprived us of half our daily allowance. On application being made for medicines for the fick, we were informed, that the ftricteft orders had been iffued not to fupply us with any; that we had not been brought there to live, and that the Nawaub would be very happy to hear we were all dead. This cruel treatment operated very forcibly on the feelings of thofe gentlemen who were at this time in a bad ftate of health: many of them feemed to defpair of a recovery, as they were to look for no affiftance but what nature might afford. Thus unhappily fituated, we ufed every means to procure fome medicines, but all in vain, for the fentries (the only perfons to whom we could apply) told us, that however much they were inclined to contribute to our relief, it was not in their power.

On the 13th, three women, who were confined with us, were decoyed out by a report

report of some fine salt fish being in the bazar: on their going out, the doors of our prison were immediately shut, and soon after, we were alarmed with horrid shrieks and the cries of murder, and could plainly hear the women call upon us for assistance; but as it was totally out of our power to afford them any, we could only deplore their situation in anxious suspence, not knowing what might be their fate: however, an hour had not elapsed before our apprehensions were agreeably relieved by their safe return, when they informed us they had been very roughly handled, and narrowly searched, and that a few pagodas, which they had found means to conceal, had been taken from them.

On the 15th, we were deprived of the bazar, nothing being brought for sale but sour milk, salt, chillies (or red pepper), tamarinds, and tobacco. About midnight, Serjeant Dobbins, of the 102d regiment, who had been ill of a fever some days, died; and when the doors of the prison were opened in the morning, we made the Wur-
dee

dee Wollah * acquainted with the circumſtance, and requeſted the corpſe might be immediately taken away, and decently interred; for we feared the putrid ſtench that aroſe from it might occaſion ſome infectious diſtemper; but, inſtead of complying with our requeſt, he told us we muſt dig a grave in the priſon, and bury him there; we then repreſented to him the offenſive inconvenience of ſuch a meaſure, as likewiſe the difficulty of doing it, having no tools for that purpoſe; to which he replied, "Dig it with your nails." However, after many humble entreaties, we at laſt gained our point; and the funeral ſervice having been read, the corpſe was tied up in a mat, and carried out of the priſon by our ſervants: after which the enemy tied a rope about the neck, and dragged it away.

On the 20th, they deprived us of the four milk, ſo that we had then nothing to ſubſiſt on but rice alone, without any other vehicle than water to carry it down. Un-

* Written alſo VERDUVALLA. Very many of the Hindoſtannee words are differently ſpelt, by different writers.

certain how this diet might agree with us, and several of the officers being sick and destitute of medicines, our situation became wretched, and our prospects dreadful, from a belief that the worst was yet to come, and our suspicions were still further increased by their taking away a few onions, which one of the gentlemen had reserved, from the time of our being deprived of the bazar, just as they were going to be boiled. Our privy began at this time to be very offensive, for those who were ill were unable to go to the outside, nor were any of us suffered to have access to it from sun-set to sun-rise, for during that time the doors of our prison were fast locked. Our cook-room, as well as the building just mentioned, was in the prison, on one side; we therefore laboured under another disagreeable inconvenience, from being in a continual smoke the greatest part of the day, while immense swarms of rats, bugs, fleas, and other kinds of vermin, constantly disturbed our nightly rest.

The

APPENDIX.

The daily infults we received from our cruel and tyrannical guards, joined to the reft of our treatment, when compared with our former fituations in life, at times depreffed our fpirits and hurt our feelings fo much, that words cannot do juftice to our fufferings: but, recollecting we were Britons, and how fhameful it was to yield to gloomy defpair, we endeavoured to refume our ufual gaiety of mind, determined, by the help of Providence, to furmount every difficulty, in hopes of future revenge.

About this time, died Lieutenant William Patterfon, of the 102d regiment. Before his body was cold, our inhuman guards rufhed in, and, vulture-like, feized upon the few remaining things belonging to him, threatening to punifh with rigour thofe gentlemen who fhould attempt to conceal any part of them. After permitting us to read the funeral fervice, the dead body was removed. We now became exceedingly anxious to learn the fituation of affairs, and punctually liftened every night to the converfation of the guard, from whom we hoped

ped to gather some intelligence, and were not disappointed: for we were frequently gratified with the most flattering and plausible accounts of the success of our army; which accounts were sometimes confirmed, and at other times contradicted, by the sentries, with whom we had frequent opportunities of conversing during the day.

We questioned them concerning our Europeans and Sepoys, who were confined in the fort, and they told us that the former were treated in the same manner as ourselves; but that the latter, with our servants, were only allowed one seer of rauggy, which is the worst grain in the country, and one pice each per day: that they were employed during the day to work as coolies, carrying stones, mud, and chunam, (mortar made of stone or shells) for erecting and repairing the enemy's works, and that in the evening, after they had finished their labour, they were confined in prison, with irons upon their legs, and their hands tied behind them.

They

They further informed us, that our Sepoys had been frequently afked to enter into the enemy's fervice, and threatened to be hanged in cafe they refufed to do fo, being told at the fame time, that all the European officers had engaged in the fervice of the Nawaub; but that our Sepoys difregarded their threats, and told them with a firm refolution, that they would fooner die, working as coolies, than enter into his fervice, and that they well knew none of the European officers would ever engage to ferve under him. This pleafing news of the fortitude and fidelity of our brave Sepoys, who were labouring under fuch cruel hardfhips, gave the utmoft fatisfaction, and confiderably lightened the burden of our own fufferings.

On the 3d of July, Dr. Carmichael, of the Bombay eftablifhment, had his irons knocked off, and was conducted below to vifit Dowlat Bhauee, who was fuddenly taken ill. The Doctor returned in the evening, and informed us that, after prefcribing for the Jemmidar, he gave him a moft excellent

excellent dinner, and made him an offer of remaining in an houfe below, which he declined. Dowlat Bhauee alfo promifed the Doctor that he fhould not again be put in irons, which was inviolably adhered to.

On the 11th of this month, died Lieutenant Auchinlech of the Company's troops: He had been long ill of a flux, and though frequent applications were made to have his irons taken off, our cruel tyrants would not confent to it; but, an hour before his death, they brought a black-fmith, and though we ftrongly folicited them not to difturb him in his laft moments, they pofitively infifted on knocking off his irons, which they effected with great pain to the poor dying man.

On the 7th of Auguft, having been told by the centinels, that a Marratta army, with a detachment of Englifh troops, was approaching to Chittledroog, our fpirits were much elated, as we could not avoid giving fome credit to the report, from the circumftance of fome of the principal men belonging

belonging to the government, coming up, and enquiring whether any of us underftood the nature of mortars, or how to cut fuzees, of which we all difclaimed any knowledge: they then called out five officers, to whom they offered confiderable commands in the Nawaub's fervice, as alfo to the reft of us, provided we would enter: but their offers were of courfe rejected with difdain.

On the 27th, our daily allowance was augmented to three pice each; and we were informed that a ceffation of arms had taken place, between the Eaft-India Company, and Tippoo Sultaun Nawaub Bahauder, that a treaty of peace was actually on foot, and that the Burrah Myar would be fent by the Jemmidar, to acquaint us with it: we waited impatiently for a confirmation of this joyful news, until five o'clock in the evening, when the Myar made his appearance, acquainted us, in a very formal manner, that peace was nearly concluded between the powers at war, that in the mean time we fhould have a bazar, and requefted to know all our wants. We were

were deluded into a firm belief of this intelligence, for five days; but, on the first of September, were undeceived by the bazar being again taken away, and the additional pice ftruck off: upon making enquiry into the caufe of this fudden change, we were told, that the Burrah Myar would fatisfy us on that head; but as he did not, at that time, pay us another vifit, we concluded it was only a pretext calculated to ferve fome particular purpofe.

On the 5th of October, our daily fubfiftence was again augmented to three pice, and the following day a bazar was fent to us, in which was ghee, (a very rancid fort of butter made from the milk of buffaloes) dholl, (a kind of peas which grow in fmall narrow pods on a fhrub,) fugar, wheat-flour, maffaullaw, (fundry forts of fpice) tobacco, limes, and vegetables.

On the 20th, the Burrah Myar a fecond time made his appearance, and we were in great expectation of receiving fome agreeable intelligence: but his errand was

only

only to enquire, whether any of us understood the method of making musket-flints, paper, or black-lead pencils, offering great rewards to any person who would instruct him in those arts.

On the 5th of November, we had the misfortune to lose Dr. Carmichael of the Bombay establishment, who had been ill for a considerable length of time, and whose death was much lamented by every gentleman in the prison. Though we found the weather in general milder here than on the sea coast, and the monsoon not near so violent, yet our prison was not proof against the rain, which came through most parts of the roof, and occasioned a dampness that brought on a slow fever, of which the greater part of us were at this time ill.

On the 4h of December, our servants, as they went to draw water, for the first time, had the opportunity of speaking to those servants attending upon the gentlemen in the other prison, from whom we had

the

the satisfaction to hear that they all enjoyed good health, and had only loft during their confinement, Mr. Browne, Quarter-mafter of the 100th regiment, Enfign Bateman of the Bombay eftablifhment, and a private foldier of the 98th regiment. At different periods we experinced various kinds of treatment, fometimes meeting with lefs feverity than at others: we had an inftance of their lenity on Chriftmas-day, when the bazar-man was directed to bring for fale abundance of fruit, fweetmeats, and vegetables, together with fome fheep, two of which were purchafed by fome of the gentlemen, who had faved money out of their daily allowance for that purpofe.

On the 3d of January, 1784, died, much regretted, Lieutenant Drew of the Bombay eftablifhment, after a painful lingering illnefs. Having the curiofity to enquire how they difpofed of the bodies of the deceafed, we were affured, by different people, that they were thrown over a precipice into a morafs, where they were devoured by tygers and vultures.

On

On the 10th, butcher's meat was allowed to be brought into the bazar, and fold in fmall quantities, in common with other articles. Our treatment was now much better than heretofore; we wanted for nothing that we could, with our fmall allowance, afford to purchafe; and as many as chofe were permitted to go to the outer yard, from fun-rife to fun-fet. From this great alteration in the behaviour of the enemy, as well as from their repeated affurances that peace was concluding, we were led to believe that the happy day would foon arrive when we fhould be freed from our fhackles, and once more enjoy the liberty of Britons.

On the 10th of February, died Lieutenant Hugh Moore, of the 98th regiment, who, fome days before his death, had been indulged with a room to himfelf, in an houfe in the outer yard, which after his deceafe, we were permitted to occupy during the day. We were now pofitively affured that peace was concluded, and that all the prifoners would be releafed in a few days,

days, which happy period we anxioufly waited for; but having been fo often deceived, we much fufpected the truth of this intelligence, notwithftanding the indulgent behaviour of the enemy.

On the 23d of March, however, all our doubts were cleared up, for early in the morning, the Wordy Wollah came with feveral black-fmiths, and informed us he had received orders from Dowlat Bhauee to knock off our irons, and to acquaint us that peace was concluded, and that we were to be releafed in a day or two. The emotions we felt on receiving this joyful and moft welcome news, joined to the pleafing fenfation of having our legs at liberty, no pen can defcribe; for a while, nothing but rejoicings and congratulations were heard re-echoing from every part of the prifon.

After we were freed from our fetters, we remained two days to get the proper ufe of our limbs; and on the 25th, in the morning, we bad adieu to our jail, and were con-

APPENDIX.

ducted to an open space of ground, just without the prison, where we had not been long, before we discovered at a distance our brother officers, who had been separated from us on our arrival at Chittledroog; and such was our eagerness to meet, that the fixed bayonet of the guard could not prevent our running several yards to embrace each other: this was a period of bliss, of which the first monarch in the world might justly have envied us; we were so drowned in joy, that for a while we forgot we were still in the hands of the enemy, but were soon recovered from our trance, by receiving orders to proceed below, which we gladly obeyed, and at about ten o'clock, arrived at the Kutchery, (a building erected for holding courts of judicature and transacting all public business in general,) where we had the inexpressible pleasure of meeting with Messrs. Gordon and Brunton, two Lieutenants of the Madras establishment, who had been taken prisoners some years before, and of seeing many other of our fellow-sufferers, both Europeans and Sepoys, but were not permitted to converse much

much with the latter. Our fervants, who had been taken from us on our arrival at Chittledroog, were delivered over to us, from whom gufhed tears of joy at the fight of their mafters. They informed us, that feveral of our flave-boys had been taken out of prifon and carried away: we now therefore demanded them to be given up to us, but could obtain no other redrefs or anfwer, than that " they were all dead."

Soon after our arrival here, we had the mortification to fee feveral bafkets of handcuffs placed before us, for the purpofe of again linking us two and two: but on making a forcible reprefentation to Dowlat Bhauee, and on figning a paper, wherein we gave our paroles of honour, for our own good behaviour, and bound ourfelves anfwerable for that of the troops, he relinquifhed his intention of making us fuffer that horrid, ignominious punifhment.— But we were not fo fuccefsful in our ftrenuous application in behalf of our brave, faithful foldiers, for they, poor fellows, were obliged to endure that cruel indignity.

As

As most of the officers and men were nearly naked, and all of us in want of shoes, we made an application for a sum of money to be advanced to us, on the Honourable Company's account, and were informed by Dowlat Bhauee, that a Buckshy (pay-master) would be sent with us, who would supply us with every thing we could have occasion for. Having been detained in the Kutchery till four o'clock in the afternoon, we were then all conducted to the burying ground, about one mile and an half distant from the fort. As soon as we halted, we all assembled together, and on relating to each other our sufferings, we found, that the officers who had been separated from us, were used in every respect in the same manner as ourselves. Messrs Gordon and Brunton had formely been confined at Seringapatam, where they were treated tolerably well, and for the first six months were not put in irons. About twenty months before our arrival at Chittledroog, they were removed with several European soldiers taken at the unfortunate action where Colonel Baillie was cut off, to that fort,

fort, where they were at firſt treated remarkably well, having meat and liquor daily ſerved out to them, excluſive of their allowance of rice and pice, and were beſides ſupplied with a plentiful bazar.

The capture of Bednore occaſioned their being treated ſomething worſe than before, but not to any degree of ſeverity, till thoſe gentlemen were detected in a correſpondence with Lord Macartney, governor of Madras, and in endeavouring to ſend a letter to us; in conſequence of this diſcovery, they were confined by themſelves in a ſmall dark room, the door of which was ſuffered to remain open only one hour during the day; irons were put on their hands, as well as their legs; they were fed on the ſweepings of the rauggy ſtorehouſe, being allowed only one ſeer each of that grain per day; they were alſo deprived of the bazar, and in every reſpect treated with the utmoſt rigour for ſome months, till the ceſſation of arms took place, at which time their irons were taken off, the door of their priſon kept open all day, and ever after uſed in the ſame manner as

we

we were. We learned from our servants, that what we heard of the guard in the beginning of July, regarding our Europeans and Sepoys, was strictly true.

On the 26th, having received no allowance of rice or pice for the preceding day, we asked for some victuals, and some hours after, a seer of rice and one pice was delivered to each person. We were amazed at, and did not know how to account for the reduction of our pittance; for, as peace was concluded, we naturally imagined our allowance would rather have been augmented than reduced; but, on making an enquiry into the cause, we were told, that the Commissioners from Madras, employed in negotiating the treaty, had stipulated for no kind of provisions for us, and that the Nawaub had sent orders to furnish us with just as much as was barely sufficient to support life.

In the evening we received intelligence from a Sepoy, who had formerly been in the English service, that Dowlat Bhauee had detained

detained fifteen of our drummers and flave-
boys, and confined them in an houfe clofe
to that where he lived; alfo, that the Jemmidar had kept back ten European foldiers,
and twenty-three Sepoys, whom he fepa-
rately confined in different parts of the
fort, and had given out that they were
dead.

This day and the 27th, feveral parties of
our European foldiers and Sepoys, from various parts of the country, joined us; and,
as foon as they could get an opportunity,
many of them fhewed their gratitude and
generofity, by fending feveral of us a little
money, which they had contrived to fave
when they were firft taken. As feveral officers obtained permiffion to vifit their men,
we learned that the Europeans had been
better ufed than we were, except at one
place, where, having only a feer of rauggy,
and one pice to fubfift on, they gave part of
that allowance for pieces of dried fheep-
fkins, which being the only fort of animal
food they could procure, they were afflicted
with the flux to fuch a degree, that out of
two

two hundred and thirty, only one hundred and thirteen furvived; and the enemy were fo rigid, as not even to allow them to wafh their hands and faces or comb their hair, for the fpace of four months. Our Sepoys were equally oppreffed in every prifon, all of them having been employed as coolies, carrying mud, ftones, and chunam, the whole 'time of their confinement, without any other allowance than one feer of rauggy and one pice to each; befides which, they were daily punifhed with ftripes, and threatened to be hanged for refufing to enter into the Nawaub's fervice, and in confequence of this cruel treatment great numbers of them died. One circumftance, with which we were made acquainted by fome of the European foldiers, fo much redounds to the honour of the Sepoys, that it ought not to pafs unnoticed.—In fome of the prifons where the Europeans and Sepoys were confined together, the latter faved money out of their daily allowance, and purchafed meat for the former, at the fame time telling them, they well knew the cuftoms of Europeans, and that they could not fubfift

without

without it. When on their march, also, they would not suffer the Europeans to carry their knapsacks, but the Sepoys took them and carried them themselves, telling the Europeans they were better able to bear the heat of the sun than they were, the climate being natural to them.

On the 28th, doolies having been provided for the sick, we began our march, guarded by an escort of sixty cavalry, and five hundred infantry, under the command of Meer Buckshy, for Ooscottah, where, as Dowlat Bhauee informed us, all the prisoners were to be collected, and where we should meet some of our own gentlemen sent from Madras, provided with money, and every other article requisite for our reception. The doolies were only four feet long, and in every respect so bad and incommodious, that no person who could possibly crawl would accept of one. Before we quitted the burying-ground, we obtained a promise to march at what hour we chose; but that promise was not adhered to, for we seldom or ever decamped before sun-rise. During the march, and after we halted,

halted, the guards were very particular in keeping the several parties separate: but the Buckshy was so good as to allow many of the Europeans to take off their irons.

We had made but few marches, before we found that rice alone had not sufficient sustenance in it to support us under the fatigues of constant marching in the sun; we therefore made a proposal to the bazar-man, to supply us with more necessaries of life out of his shop, at the rate of four pagodas for one, to be paid him on our arrival at Oofcottah, to which, after much entreaty, he seemingly with reluctance consented; but he exacted such an extravagant price for every article, that we did not receive more than the value of half a rupee for every four pagodas; however, that was a matter of very little consequence, when put in consideration with the preservation of our lives.

Nothing further material happened till our arrival at Seerahungy, on the 8th of April, when the Buckshy informed us, he expected a gentleman high in the Company's ny's civil service at Madras, would overtake us that night, as he had heard he was very near; and the next morning, before the rear had marched off the ground, the gentleman alluded to, and Ensign Fomblong, of the same establishment, overtook us. The appearance of these gentlemen gave us inexpressible satisfaction, for nothing could be more agreeable to us, at this time, than meeting with some of our own countrymen. Those gentlemen who were in the rear were very cordially received by Mr. Fomblong; but the other English gentleman's conduct was not so pleasing, for though he had it much in his power to have assisted us if he had chosen it, when he was requested by one of the officers to use his endeavours with the Buckshy, to have all the men taken out of irons, he replied, *" the situation " the troops were then in was the best and se- " curest way of marching them."*

Another officer represented to this gentleman the many distresses of the officers and men, and particularly mentioned their being bare-footed, as also the necessity we
were

were reduced to of purchasing the mere necessaries of life from the bazar-man, at such an exorbitant interest. In answer to which, this gentleman told him, he could give us no assistance; he and asked him, how he intended to discharge the bazar debt? Then immediately turning to another officer, with the coolest indifference, he asked him what corps he belonged to. The officer who addressed this gentleman in behalf of himself and fellow-sufferers, was so shocked at those words, and his behaviour, that he could make him no answer, but took his leave in silent astonishment.

This extraordinary behaviour in a gentleman who possessed ample means of doing us service, hurt our feelings more sensibly than any thing we had hitherto experienced.— Such treatment from the enemy might, in some degree, have been expected; but to receive it from one of our own countrymen, and from the first person, too, who was an eye-witness of our distress, was cruel beyond measure. Allowing, what indeed but too plainly appeared, that this gentleman did

not

not poffefs much of the milk of human nature, yet furely fuch a fcene of diftrefs might have provoked some fparks of compaffion, efpecially as the affiftance he might have procured for us, would have coft him no more than a bare application to the perfon under whofe charge we then were. After a fhort ftay, this gentleman and Enfign Fomblong proceeded on their way to Bangalore, the former leaving us a prefent of fix bottles and an half of various forts of liquors, which our fituation did not allow us to refufe, as we concluded it might be of fervice to fome of our companions who were fick.

On the 12th, having loft, by death, only two Europeans, we arrived at Oofcottah, where we found Lieutenant Dallas, of the Madras cavalry, who had been appointed by the commiffioners to receive the prifoners. Mr. Dallas's behaviour was widely different from that of the gentleman, whofe conduct I have been relating. The contraft was a very pleafing one, for Mr. Dalls came to us in the evening, accompanied by Lieutenant M'Alliftor

M'Alliftor and Cornet Lennard, of the Madras cavalry, and with the moft friendly good nature, offered every affiftance he was able to afford us.

On the 13th, another party of prifoners arrived, whom the Commiffioners had collected on their march from Mangalore, when a fecond happy meeting enfued, and in the evening we all joined Lieutenant Dallas, and were delivered over in change to Beem Row, a Bramin appointed by the Nawaub to conduct the Britifh prifoners from Oofcottah to the Carnatic. We now enjoyed a greater fcope of liberty, than we had ever done fince we were captured, being allowed to range over the whole camp; and Beem Row was fo good as to take all the troops out of irons, though he had orders to the contrary: we alfo lived in perfect luxury, compared to our late mode of exifting, for Mr. Dallas furnifhed us with tents, and daily fupplied us with meat and liquors; and ufed all his exertions to give general fatisfaction. This day arrived from Bangalore Mr. Sadlier, and Colonel Braith-

Braithwaite, of the Madras eftablifhment, which latter gentleman obtained permiffion from the Nawaub to proceed to Madras, with Mr. Sadlier, before the other prifoners: they accordingly fet out for the Carnatic the next morning, leaving a large quantity of the Company's liquors, and two thoufand pagodas, which fum was afterwards diftributed, referving a part for the other prifoners, who were hourly expected: each of the officers received two pagodas, each of the failors one pagoda and an half, and each foldier one pagoda; the Sepoys did not receive any until fome days after, when they each fhared one rupee and an half. Each of the officers alfo received a hat, a pair of fhoes, four pair of ftockings, and a fufficient quantity of broad cloth for one coat; thefe articles having been fent up by the Government of Madras.

APPENDIX.

APPENDIX.

C.

Prison Song in Seringapatam.

I.

YE folks of Madras,
Who your time gaily pass,
Unheedful of sorrow's sad tale;
Could you list to my song,
You'd not think it wrong
To take a short peep at our Jail;
The writer so merry,
The stiff secretary,
The gorger on turkey and ham,
Not doom'd to relieve,
Might laugh in his sleeve
At his friends in Seringapatam.

II.

But, firſt, could you gueſs
Our whimſical dreſs,
Or ſhould I the matter diſcloſe;
I fear, on my life,
Whether maiden or wife,
Your ladies might cock up their noſe:
Shirt, jacket and trowzers,
And chains, curſed rowzers,
Which oft we eternally damn,
The chief dreſs compoſe
Of your priſon-pent beaux,
In jail at Seringapatam.

III.

Nor let me refuſe,
Like an ill-natur'd muſe,
But gladly include in my taſk,
So worthy of lays,
Let me ſing the loud praiſe
Of the ſagely-contriv'd gally-gaſs:,
Ceaſe Pinchley, to crack,
With your friend at your back,
Your inventions are all but a ſham
To this guard o' the ſkin,
On each ſhambling ſhin,
In chains at Seringapatam.

IV.

Some fops of the place,
With ſcraps of dull lace,

Their old batter'd beavers bedeck;
  Whilſt with patches of red
  Some their jackets beſpread,
For want of a cuff or a neck:
  In huge moorman's ſlippers,
  Not unlike Dutch ſkippers,
Some make a moſt graceful ſalam;
  Whilſt ſome with their toes
  Sticking out of their ſhoes
Trudge the jail of Seringapatam.

V.

At breakfaſt our food
  Might not appear good,
Compar'd with your toaſt and your tea;
  Yet the praiſes I'll utter
  Of conjee and butter,
Or hoppers well fried in good ghee.
  We've thick ſour tyre *,
  What can we deſire,
And all for a golden fanam:
  We've milk and we've rice,
  And we've every thing nice,
In the jail of Seringapatam.

VI.

For dinner we uſe
  The moſt delicate ſtews,

* Sour milk.

Serv'd up in a new-fashion'd style;
   Yet when in a hurry
   Dispense with a curry,
Tho' sometimes we've roast and we've boil'd:
   No pinch'd pitty-patty,
   Each man has his chatty
Of high-flavour'd goat or of ram,
   Then drinks in pure water
   Wife, Mistress, or Daughter:
The toast at Seringapatam.

VII.

   Then could you but see
   Our afternoon's tea,
Your customs to better must yield;
   Nor would you sip long
   Your slop of Souchong,
But fly to the herb of the field;
   When jaggary syrup
   We mix and we stir up,
Convinc'd you'd surrender the palm,
   And strike off old Hyson,
   That nervous flow poison,
For tea of Seringapatam.

VIII.

   Some sly saving cubs,
   By hoarding their dubs,
I'll warrant old hands at that trade;
   Oft indulge in a swinger
   Of nice preserv'd ginger,
Or orange in rich marmalade:

Our evenings we pass,
Like the gay at Madras,
With Whist, with Spadille, and with Pam,
    Cheroot *, hubble-bubble,
    Then smother our trouble
In jail at Seringapatam.

IX.

Each temperate day
With health glides away,
No triflings † our forenoons profane;
    We kick up our cruppers
    At high-seafon'd suppers,
Which sleep from our eyes might detain:
    Yet some with disgrace
    Have bepimpled their face
By decoction of doll or of gram,
    Or the high plantain fritter,
    For freedom much fitter
Than jail at Seringapatam.

X.

Nor here be forgot
Our neat bamboo cot,
Unpainted, uncarv'd, and unguilt;
    Nor that best of all rugs,
    When divested of bugs,
Which we find in a beggarman's quilt:
    We lay ourselves flat
    On a clean three-dub mat,

* Cheroot is tobbacco rolled up in Sagars,
† Luncheons.

Our pillows with ſtraw we do cram ;
We find ſweet repoſe,
Often freed from our foes,
Oft releas'd from Seringapatam.

XI.

You'd think we were far gone
To hear but the jargon
Of nations ſo ſtrangely combin'd;
We've Danes and we've Dutchmen,
You ſcarce have ſeen ſuch men,
And ſcarcely again will you find :
We've Sawneys and Paddies,
And braw Highland laddies,
Free Britons in here too they ramm;
The Swiſs and the Frenchman,
The leek-loving Welchman,
All chain'd in Seringapatam.

XII.

Each trade, each profeſſion,
In various progreſſion,
You'd find in our priſon's ſmall round;
We've carpenters, taylors,
We've ſnuffmen, and ſailors,
And ſage politicians profound:
The lawyer, phyſician,
The cruel muſician,
The good Commandant Sid Abram;
The painter, the poet,
The great wit, the no wit,
All, all in Seringapatam.

The

XIII.

The Muſſulmans *baut**
Is extenſively taught,
Nor paſs we our days like dull ſots;
With a ſtone for a ſcraper,
Deny'd pen and paper,
We write on the fragments of pots:
We've books few in number,
But not like your lumber
Our ſhelves do they uſeleſsly jamm;
Each night in the guard,
Leſt we ſtudy too hard,
They're ſecur'd, in Seringapatam†.

XIV.

Some ſweet recreation,
Each day in rotation,
The ſadneſs of each doth amuſe;
Nor like Wiſe Men of *Gotum*,
Reject we Tee-totum,
Chuck marbles, or Game of the Gooſe;
Some roar the loud ſong,
" To Anacreon;"

---

* Language of Moors.

† So ſuperſtitious and abſurd was their dread of Europeans, though in priſon, and ſo extravagant the notions they entertained of our art and knowledge, that they were apprehenſive leſt, if the few books we had ſhould be left in our hands in the night time, we might in ſome unlucky hour, by means of ſome ſpells or enchantments, in which they might be inſtrumental, contrive to make our eſcape, or to overcome our guards and deſtroy the priſon

More piously some raise a Psalm;
Some rattle the dice,
Some catch rats and mice,
In jail at Seringapatam.

XV.

Still thus let's disguise
Our sadness and sighs,
Thus chace away chilly despair;
Resign'd to our woes,
And the chains of our foes,
Submit to the soldier's hard fare;
Let's think each to-morrow
Must shorten our sorrow,
Let hope serve instead of a dram,
That freedom once more
May open the door
Of our Jail at Seringapatam.

APPENDIX.

D.

Prison Song in Bangalore.

I.

AT length now that liberty dawns,
The Muse who lay dormant so long;
Companion to mis'ry in bonds,
Upraises her head with a song.
 To you our old friends in Madras,
Who surely our suff'rings bewail;
 While your hours so cheerfully pass,
View the scenes of our Bangalore jail.

II.

In affluence rolling at ease,
You've nothing to hope or to fear;
 You live and you rove as you please,
Unconscious of what passes here.
 Retire then from pleasure and play,
And list to our sorrowful tale;
 Regard not the news of the day,
While we shew you our Bangalore jail.

III.

How can we be cheerful and gay,
When hunger affails us fo keen;
How can we with fix cafh a day,
Repel the invafion of fpleen?
In vain our hard fate we repine,
In vain on our fortunes we rail;
On Mullaga Tony we dine,
Or Conjee, in Bangalore jail.

IV.

Like horfes we're pent in a fhade,
Like felons we're loaded with chains;
And while mother earth is our bed,
We float in the time of the rains.
The centinels plac'd at the door,
Are for our fecurity bail;
With mufkets and chaubucks fecure,
They guard us in Bangalore jail.

V.

Along the Veranda we ftalk,
And think on paft pleafure with pain;
With arms enfolded we walk,
And figh for thofe pleafures again.
And oft is our thinking confin'd,
To means of projecting a meal;
Which if we effect to our mind,
We're happy in Bangalore jail.

VI.

VI.

As famine approaches our gate,
More faving we grow in our fare;
 Refolv'd to encounter our fate,
We bury the thoughts of defpair.
 We feel with regret our decay,
So meagre, fo lank, and fo pale;
 Like gholts we are rang'd in array,
When mufter'd in Bangalore jail.

VII.

Then while the beft days of our prime,
Walk flowly and wretchedly on;
 We pafs the dull hours of our time
With marbles, cards, dice, or a fong;
 While others fit mending their clothes,
Which long fince began for to fail;
 Amufements that lighten the woes
Of the captive in Bangalore jail.

VIII.

The doctor, with joy in his face,
Arrives with a timely fupply;
 He brings the glad tidings of peace,
And that our releafement is nigh.
 Since freedom to vifit us deigns,
In raptures we open the mail;
 Difcordant we rattle our chains,
The mufic of Bangalore jail.

[300]

APPENDIX.

E.

Prison Expences of Seringapatam

Expences of fitting up a Prisoner newly arrived at Seringapatam.

	F.	D.	C.
ONE piece of coarse cloth, which makes two shirts	4	5	0
Chints for one jacket	2	0	0
Lining for ditto	1	0	0
Moorman's slippers	1	3	0
Leather and tape for galligaskins *	0	3	0
Beggarman's quilt, of old rags †	1	0	0
Mat to sleep on	0	3	0
Straw for pillows	0	1	0
Basket for clothes	0	5	0
An earthen chatty to eat off	0	0	2
One earthen bason, 2 goglets	0	3	0
A china or wooden spoon	0	2	0
Half piece of Dungeree, for pillow-cases, towels, &c.	1	6	3
A long drawer string	0	1	0
A wooden comb	0	0	2
Jaggary Pot (molasses)	0	0	1
Broom	0	0	1
Lamp	0	0	0½
Tape to queau hair	0	1	0
	13	2	0½

* The galligaskins are made of leather, and wore under the irons to preserve the skin.

† A beggarman's quilt was a garment made of rags, collected from all hands, and of all colours, washed and sewed together. It was warm and comfortable, though an object of laughter.

Articles

APPENDIX.

Articles of Luxury, only to be obtained by the Opulent after a Length of Saving.

	F.	D.	C.
ONE common knife - - -	1	0	0
One pen ditto - - - - -	0	9	0
One comley, as a covering - -	4	6	0
Bamboos and ropes for a cot - -	1	2	0
Bamboos for ... - - - -	0	8	0
Paper per ... - - - -	0	1	2
Reeds for pens, each - - -	0	0	1
Sweetmeats, per stick - - -	0	0	1
Six plaintains - - - -	0	1	0
Six limes - - - - -	0	1	0
Four ... - - - - -	0	1	0
Six guavas - - - - -	0	1	0
Three mangoes - - - -	0	1	0
Eight cheroots - - - -	0	1	0
Tobacco in stalk (reed for smoking) -	0	0	0½
Dressing a hubble-bubble per week, at three chillums * per day (three or four)	0	3	0
Keeping a pair of pigeons, per week -	0	1	2
Paint, paper, paste, &c. for making a pack of cards - - - - -	0	9	0
Ditto for making back-gammon table -	0	2	0
Ivory for one pair of dice - - -	0	5	0
Chess-board of paper, and men - -	0	8	3

* CHILLUMS are balls of tobacco and plantains, and certain spices.

APPENDIX.

One Week's Expence for a Mess of Eight Gentlemen: Breakfast and Dinner.

MONDAY. Cutcheree.	Fana.	Dubs.	Cath.	TUESDAY. Fowl Curry.	Fana.	Dubs.	Cath.
Four loaves bread	0	9	0	Bread	0	9	0
Milk	0	2	1	Milk	0	2	1
Butter	0	4	2	Butter	0	4	0
Burnt rice, as a substitute for coffee	0	1	0	Rice-coffee	0	1	0
				Four fowls	2	0	0
				Curry stuff	0	3	2
Rice	0	7	0	Two seer rice	0	7	0
Doll	0	3	0	Ghee	0	7	3
Ghee	0	9	0	Greens	0	0	0
Onions	0	3	0	Chatties	0	2	0
Cloves, &c.	0	1	0	Wood	0	4	0
Wood	0	4	0				
Salt	0	1	0				
Total	4	0	3	Total	5	8	0

WEDNESDAY. Mutton Curry.	Fana.	Dubs.	Cath.	THURSDAY. Mutton Baked.	Fana.	Dubs.	Cath.
Bread	0	9	0	Bread	0	9	0
Milk	0	2	1	Milk	0	2	1
Butter	0	4	0	Butter	0	4	0
Rice-coffee	0	1	0	Rice-coffee	0	1	0
One quarter mutton	1	1	2	Muttton 2 quarters	2	2	1
Rice	0	7	2	Greens	0	3	0
Curry stuff	0	3	2	Spices	0	2	0
Ghee	0	5	0	Pepper	0	2	0
Greens	0	0	3	Salt	0	1	0
Wood	0	4	0	Wood	0	4	0
Total	4	5	2	Total	6	5	2

FRIDAY.

APPENDIX.

FRIDAY. Doll Pepper Water.	Fana.	Dubs.	Cath.	SATURDAY. Fowl Curry.	Fana.	Dubs.	Cath.
Bread - -	0	9	0	Bread - -	0	9	0
Milk - -	0	2	1	Milk - -	0	2	1
Butter - -	0	4	0	Butter - -	0	4	0
Rice-coffee -	0	1	0	Rice-coffee -	0	1	0
Doll - -	0	3	0	Four fowls -	2	0	0
Rice - -	0	7	2	Ghee - -	1	2	0
Curry stuff -	0	3	2	Curry stuff -	0	8	2
Ghee - -	0	4	0	Onions - -	0	3	0
Wood - -	0	4	0	Rice - -	0	7	2
				Wood - -	0	4	0
				Chilleys - -	0	2	0
Total	3	5	1	Total	6	4	1

SUNDAY. Mutton Curry.	Fana.	Dubs.	Cath.	TOTAL EXPENCES OF THE WEEK.	Fana.	Dubs.	Cath.
Bread - -	0	9	0	Monday - -	4	0	3
Butter - -	0	4	0	Tuesday - -	5	8	0
Milk - -	0	2	1	Wednesday -	4	5	2
Rice-coffee -	0	1	0	Thursday -	6	5	2
Mutton - -	1	2	0	Friday - -	3	5	1
Rice - -	0	7	2	Saturday -	6	4	1
Ghee - -	0	5	0	Sunday - -	4	7	0
Curry stuff -	0	3	2				
Wood - -	0	4	0	Total	35	3	1
Greens - -	0	0	3				
				Received from Hyder -	56	0	0
Total	4	7	1				

By

By the above calculation, each gentleman shares two gold fanams and seven dubs per week; and there remains three dubs and three cash in the caterer's hands towards the expences of the week ensuing.— This surplus, from being laid out in Pia arrack in the early age of this society, obtained, and still goes by the name of Arrack Money, and is our only fund for clothes, payment of a fanam per month each to a washerman, medicines, and the incidental expences of jaggary, oil, soap, limes, thread, needles, tape, chatties, public subscriptions, &c. &c. The fanam changes for eleven dubs and four cash; one dub, eleven fanams, one pagoda.

www.ingramcontent.com/pod-product-compliance
Lightning Source LLC
Chambersburg PA
CBHW022058230426
43672CB00008B/1214